BERMUDA
IN 5 HOURS

PAN AMERICAN
AIRWAYS

IMPERIAL
AIRWAYS

The ART
of the
AIRWAYS

GEZA SZUROVY

ZENITH
PRESS

Library of Congress Cataloging-in-Publication Data Available
ISBN 978-0-7603-1395-4

Edited by Sara Perfetti
Designed by LeAnn Kuhlmann

Printed in Hong Kong

On the front cover: P. G. Lawler's interpretation of Pacific bliss Pan American style is one of the best-known aviation posters of the 1930s. It shows a Boeing 314 landing in the bay at Pago Pago, the most challenging seaplane base in Pan American's Pacific network.

On the endpapers, front: Late 1950s KLM route map.

On the frontis page: By the late 1930s Pan American provided regular service to Bermuda. Imperial Airways is also featured, indicative of the hope of bridging the Atlantic with Imperial flying the British sector. But transatlantic service to Britain had to wait because British flying boats lacked the range for regular service and the airline was forbidden by government policy to buy non-British aircraft.

On the title page: Air France was one of the first airlines to connect the United States with Europe after World War II. This 1948 poster by Maurus entices affluent American tourists to visit the Old World.

On the endpapers, back: 1937 Air France route map.

On the back cover: Left: Spain was one of TWA's most popular destinations. David Klein's portrait captures the tension in the arena as the matador parades to face death in the afternoon. **Right, top:** This poster celebrates the first crossing of the south Atlantic. It was achieved in 1930 by Aeropostale's Jean Mermoz and his crew in a Latécoère 28 on floats. **Middle:** Southern California's playground beckons and the best way to get there is in a United DC-6 from this 1950s poster. **Two posters on lower right:** Two Transcontinental and Western Airlines posters from a rare set of lithographs featuring the world's first pressurized airliner, the four-engined Boeing 307 Stratoliner.

CONTENTS

ACKNOWLEDGMENTS   6

INTRODUCTION   7

1   FUR COATS AND FOOT WARMERS   10

2   GOING GLOBAL   46

3   PROPLINER SPLENDOR   86

4   CONTRAILS AROUND THE WORLD   134

INDEX   178

*A*rt of the Airways is the result of a rewarding blend of traditional research in museums, libraries, and airline archives, and a grassroots effort using the Internet to connect and network with private collectors, who are also important caretakers of this field of airline history.

First I'd like to pay tribute to the memory of Don Thomas, whose three books on airline poster art and publicity memorabilia I've been thumbing through regularly for many years. Don's love of such artwork and his dedication to its preservation, evident in his books, inspired me to start an airline poster collection of my own.

Since my own poster collection falls short of filling a book, I contacted many traditional sources and then wandered onto eBay, the virtual auction house on the Internet, which proved to be a revelation. With a few clicks of the mouse I found myself looking at 181 airline posters, ranging from the 1920s to the present. Many of them were valuable collectors' items, regularly seen in auction houses and poster galleries. I became an eBay addict, tempted daily by an ever-changing lot of posters to enhance my own collection. More importantly, it led me to other collectors.

I am especially indebted to two private collectors I met on eBay, Arik Bendorf and Dubi Silverstein. Arik specializes mostly in Pan American posters and airline posters of Hawaii. Dubi casts a wider net, looking primarily for powerful images. His collection includes nice selections of Air France, United, American, Northwest Orient, SAS, TWA, and Pan American posters among others. A substantial number of the posters in this book come from these two collections.

Along traditional lines I'd like to thank Lufthansa and Air France, two particularly cooperative airlines. Air France has done the most among all airlines to preserve its posters, maintaining a collection of more than 350 of them. Thanks are also due to the Hungarian Museum of Transportation and its director, Dr. Katona András; my mother, Thea Sambuchi Bless, for making the connection; and to the British Airways Museum for showing me the collection saved from oblivion by its dedicated volunteers. Thanks to London's Science Museum; the Museum of Flight in Seattle, Washington; and the Quadrant Picture Library's Flight Collection, where curator Paul Gladman found rare photographs of early airliners to help put the posters in perspective.

I am also indebted to John Pothecary in England for two of the rarest posters, Martin Berinstein, George Antoniades, Terry Primak, Lyn Markey, and others for letting me disrupt their wall decor, and editors Mike Haenggi and Sara Perfetti at MBI Publishing Company without whom this book would have remained wishful thinking.

AIR FRANCE
AMÉRIQUE DU SUD

This poster by the op artist Vasarely of an Air France Constellation winging its way toward Rio de Janeiro's Sugarloaf after a long flight across the South Atlantic is an example of a fine artist venturing into the world of commercial poster art with rewarding results.

I never gave much thought to the South Pacific until I saw P. G. Lawler's poster of the Pan American flying boat landing in the bay at Pago Pago (seen on page 83). As I absorbed the idyllic scene I sensed the silky warmth of the sun's first rays, the sweet scent of frangipani, the rustling palm leaves, and the old Pan Am Clipper whistling down final approach, its four tired engines throttled back to a low purr at journey's end. In seconds there would be the reassuring slap of hull on water, a last burst of power to the jetty, and the eerie silence that comes on arrival after droning through the inky, starry night. And then would come breakfast on the beach, in a drowsy, agreeable daze, to the murmur of the morning tide. I knew then that I had to go there. And I did.

Four decades after Pan American's last flying boat was gone that old poster was still doing its job, enticing the viewer to distant lands. Pan American was not flying to the South Pacific at that time but it did get me from San Francisco to Hawaii, the first Pacific destination its flying boats had pioneered in the 1930s. We flew there in another Pan Am relic, one of the first Boeing 747 jumbo jets that its pushy founder, Juan Trippe, had personally cajoled Boeing into building. Then it was on to islands scattered far to the south, on a gracefully aging Hawaiian Airlines Douglas DC-8. And at the right moment, on the right morning, the idyll was just as P. G. Lawler had promised.

Airline posters have been luring travelers ever since the world's first airline, the St. Petersburg-Tampa Airboat Line, pasted up its modest announcement in 1914 offering "fast passenger and express service" between the two cities. Much more extravagant posters would soon follow as other, more enduring airlines extended their reach across the world, for the poster was the most powerful visual advertising medium before the age of color television and glossy consumer magazines. Thousands of airline poster designs have been created over the years, and those that survive leave us a rich visual history of airline travel in aviation's century.

Art of the Airways brings together a collection of these posters to evoke the past they represent. It includes images most coveted by art collectors whose primary criteria for valuing airline posters are rarity, production method, image quality, age, and the artist's reputation. But primarily it features a wider selection of posters valued as much or more for the airline history they portray. It opens with the energetic, adventurous period from the early 1900s to the outbreak of World War II when the airlines rapidly expanded from modest beginnings to encircle the globe. It then presents in detail for the first time one of the most prolific eras of the airliner poster, the age of the great propliners during the 1950s, the time when air travel matured into a common form of transportation. It continues on to the early

In 1937 Transcontinental and Western Air was quick to put the DC-3 into service in both day and sleeper versions. The DC-3's institutionalized reliable transcontinental air service provided a truly viable faster alternative to going by train.

jet age, the launch of the era of mass air travel, which had its own share of captivating posters. It concludes with a handful of more modern posters, several of which come full circle to commemorate air travel's young history.

The origin of the color poster predates the appearance of the earliest aviation posters by only about thirty years. Posters pioneered mass advertising beginning in the 1880s, when the industrial revolution created the first consumer societies among the rapidly growing urban populations of Europe and America. The period coincided with the perfection of color lithography by Jules Cheret, which made possible the production of color images in large numbers. These color posters were stone lithographs, expensive and technically challenging to make, but affordable enough for companies to commission print runs of as many as 2,000 to 3,000 copies.

Cheret's technique fixed the image in reverse on a flat porous stone with an acid process. When the stone was inked and washed, the ink stuck only to the fixed image. The paper sheet was then pressed onto the stone and absorbed the inked image. Several stones were used, each inked with different colors to achieve the desired effect as the paper was pressed in sequence onto each stone. According to the London Transport Museum, a poster using eight colors and printed in 1,000 copies required 8,000 separate workshop procedures and took several weeks to produce. The variations were endless, the results stunningly rich in color and texture. When the print run was completed the image was cleared off and the stone was reused. Reprints were not an option.

The vibrant posters were pasted up on billboards and the tall, round municipal stands specially designed to display them; they attracted admirers by the thousands in Paris, London, Berlin, New York, and other urban centers. They hawked every conceivable product, service, and political agenda including the joys of absinthe, light bulbs, automobiles, rail and ship travel, the French Riviera, the London Underground, and the Russian Revolution. International air meets became a favored topic in the early 1900s, soon followed by advertisements to travel by air.

Stone lithographs predominated until the late 1930s when perfected photochemical and mechanical printing processes pushed them out in favor of the inexpensive offset color print and silk screening, reprintable on demand. But the print runs of airline posters remained relatively small as most were displayed in the airlines' ticket offices and distributed to the travel agencies representing them. As a poster image became obsolete for advertising use, the agencies and airlines threw it out and it went out of print. Fortunately posters of every era had their admirers even in their time, who squirreled them away in varying numbers.

When aircraft were the revolutionary and somewhat dangerous new way to go, the posters prominently featured them, harping on their speed, and rather disingenuously emphasizing their comfort to tempt passengers off the plush long-distance trains. But the allure of exotic destinations was a strong draw from the beginning, and as airline safety improved and speed was taken for granted the destination became the dominant theme. The aircraft image became smaller and smaller and eventually vanished from most posters.

In artistic style airline posters generally followed period trends. The frilly, nature-inspired Art Nouveau influence is evident among the first attempts at conveying the advantages of flying. In the early 1900s in Germany advertising's specific needs led to the development of Poster style, the representation of the simple, powerful brand image, such as Lufthansa's crane symbol, which remains the airline's emblem to this day. The clean, streamlined Art Deco style of the 1920s and 1930s that celebrated speed, power, and the machine, and was in part inspired by the achievements of aviation, seemed made for advertising air travel. Following World War II airline posters ranged freely across a mélange of styles, from the realistic portrayal of destination scenes to the abstract images of various modern art movements.

Poster work was the bread and butter of many commercial graphic artists. Some remained anonymous, but a handful became famous for their posters, often hired to do a whole series for a company. Many of these artists created posters for a wide range of products and services and also worked as magazine and book illustrators. Their commissions for the airlines were only a small part of their work.

Albert Solon, Otto Arpke, Maurus, Guy Arnoux, A. M. Cassandre, Jean Carlu, Paul Colin, Jan Wijga, and Lucien Boucher all rose to prominence in Europe between the two world wars, though several of them created airline posters throughout their careers, stretching into the 1950s and 1960s. America's P. G. Lawler is renown for his Pan American posters of the 1930s. E. McKnight Kauffer, another American, did most of his commercial work in London, but returned to the United States in 1940 and did several well-known posters for American Airlines and Pan American in subsequent years.

Other American artists whose posters were popular during the propliner and early jet eras include Galli and Feher, both noted for their work for United, and Weimer Pursell and Aaron Fine. David Klein is becoming particularly well known among collectors for his prolific series commissioned by TWA to promote its transition to jets.

In Europe, Bernard Villemot, Nathan, and Guy Georget were all commissioned to do series for Air France, the most enthusiastic user of posters among the airlines from the 1940s through the 1970s. Frank Wootton's work for British Overseas Airways Corporation carried on the traditions of the great Imperial Airways posters. Otto Nielsen created an evocative worldwide destination series for Scandinavian Airlines System in the 1950s and 1960s. Occasionally even fine art artists, such as Vasarely, couldn't resist the financial rewards of an airline poster commission.

Beginning in the late 1950s the airline art poster uneasily coexisted with the color photo poster and eventually gave way as color photography and large-format photo reproduction improved. The photographs may have more effectively conveyed the message to an audience increasingly hooked on glossy color photo magazines and interested in photographs of potential destinations, however idealized. But deprived of the artist's unconstrained freedom to create, interpret, symbolize, and exaggerate, most of them lacked the enduring power and variety of the best art posters, and in the end they, too, faded from the scene.

Today, when many of the airlines that commissioned posters are gone and contemporary airline posters are mostly restricted to the occasional commemorative print, vintage airline posters are becoming increasingly collectible. Most prized are the old stone lithographs dating back to before World War II. The rarest among them can command tens of thousands of dollars at auction and many go for thousands. Increasingly valued are the many posters from the propliner era of the 1950s as the period fades from recent memory into history. And even the posters of the early jet age, the last great airliner poster era, are steadily rising in price and finding their way into the

An evocative image of the Spanish airline Lineas Aereas Postales Espanolas, depicting a trimotor over Spain's arid northern mountains as it shuttled mail to France and points beyond. LAPE was a forerunner of Spain's national airline, Iberia.

showrooms of the top poster dealers and auction houses.

While prices are rising, the good news is that anyone can afford to enjoy the art of airline posters at some level. Many of the early posters are widely available in modern, high-quality reproductions, of no value to the serious art collector, but a visual treat for any nostalgia buff. The more recent posters are as affordable as a meal at a top restaurant. Going back further in time, the price steadily climbs, but many of the outstanding posters of the 1930s can still be acquired for no more than a fancy home entertainment system. It is a matter of priorities for most of us—and the allure of the past.

FUR COATS AND FOOT WARMERS

First the ground staff handed the young woman a pair of fleece-lined flying boots and a full-length sheepskin coat. Then she was given a fur-lined leather helmet, gloves, and a pair of flying goggles. She struggled into the heavy, awkward flying attire, and when she was ready to board, two burly men grabbed her by the feet and shoulders and unceremoniously lifted her into the Handley Page 0/400's circular open cockpit in front of the pilot's compartment. The woman was Freya Stark, soon to be a best-selling author admired for her long, solitary travels throughout the exotic Near East, but on that day in 1922 she was embarking on her first airline flight. The towering twin-engined contraption resembling a box-kite was about to fly her from London's Croydon Airport to Paris, Le Bourget.

Stark shared her tiny cockpit with the navigator. Soon they were underway in a maelstrom of wind, hanging on to the cockpit stringers in the turbulence as best they could in the absence of seatbelts. They flew low enough to watch a fox lope across a field as Kent's green mosaic countryside floated past below them at a leisurely ninety miles per hour. The navigator shouted out the names of the towns below, but the wind swept away his words. Like most of the first airliners in the immediate aftermath of World War I, their Handley Page was a converted bomber. Stark could have ridden in its enclosed main cabin, which carried fourteen passengers in wicker chairs, but she chose to maximize the thrill, and, anyway, she would have had almost as much need for the sheepskin flying gear inside the drafty, freezing fuselage.

They arrived at Le Bourget on schedule in a little over two hours. By surface transportation the trip would have taken all day.

Passenger comforts being minimal at the airport, Stark had to cadge a mirror from a customs official to reconstruct her disheveled hairdo before taking the complimentary airline limousine into central Paris. Stark would live to travel on jets, but decades later she wrote that she never enjoyed any other air journey as much as that first trip.

While Stark's flight was a pioneering adventure for 1922, the earliest experiments with commercial air transportation preceded it by over a decade when DELAG, the German Airship Transport Company, attempted to connect Germany's major cities by Zeppelin airship service. Initially the challenge of maintaining flight schedules proved too great for the awkward dirigibles, but they succeeded in attracting people by the thousands for local sightseeing flights. By the time the outbreak of World War I shut them down they had carried more than 10,000 fare-paying passengers on more than 1,500 flights without a single injury.

The first scheduled airplane service is generally acknowledged to have been established on the other side of the Atlantic, in Florida, by the St. Petersburg-Tampa Airboat Line in January 1914. The route was an inspired choice, because alternatively travelers could either chug across Tampa Bay in coastal steamers or travel around it by train on a journey that could take as many as twelve hours. The St. Petersburg-Tampa Airboat Line's plucky two-seat Benoist flying boats cut the crossing to thirty minutes. The line maintained its schedule reliably, but with space for only one passenger per flight and opposition from local steamship and railroad interests it lasted only through the three months of its initial municipal contract.

Effective airline building had to wait until the aftermath of World War I, and found its roots in Europe, where conditions favored the emergence of the first airlines that would endure. Europe's railroad system was decimated by the war. Distances between major cities were relatively short. Natural barriers such as the English Channel required long, tedious surface crossings making travelers receptive to a swifter, if seemingly risky, alternative. And during the war European airplane makers had accumulated enough experience with large, multi-engined bombers—such as the French Farman Goliath, the German Gotha, and the British Handley Page—to readily convert them into airliners capable of carrying as many as fourteen passengers.

German, French, British, and Dutch lines predominated, but airlines were also popping up in most other countries throughout the continent. Many were shoestring operations, short on capital and long on romance. Some were backed by well-established transport companies such as the Hapag Lloyd shipping line, which saw potential synergy with the new age way to travel. Others, such as Handley Page Transport and Junkers Luftverkehr, were formed by the aircraft makers that built their fleets.

London–Paris was the most glamorous route, capturing the lion's share of publicity. The contending French and British airlines vied to attract celebrities, strove to outdo each other on such amenities as five-course champagne lunch flights, promoted shopping weekends in Paris, and spent liberally to style their interiors and service standards to measure up to their chief competitor, the Pullman train. By 1922 there were five companies chasing the handful of daily passengers on the route.

But while the London–Paris route got all the attention, important achievements were being realized elsewhere in Europe's emerging airline network. The world's first sustained airline service was started in Germany by Deutsche Luft Reederei in 1919 between Berlin and Weimar. By the early 1920s a spider web of routes, longer and more traveled than any in Europe, connected all major German cities with scheduled services. Its workhorse was the Junkers F-13, the world's first modern, all-metal airliner.

In the south of France, Toulouse-based Lignes Aériennes G. Latécoère was flying down into Spain and across to Casablanca, Morocco, in North Africa as early as 1919, mostly carrying mail on its 850-mile route that took thirty hours with ten interim stops. The service laid the foundations of Latécoère's ambitions to push on across the Sahara to Dakar, Senegal, and establish a South American mail service that would be linked by a transatlantic route.

Air Union meanwhile linked northern France with the playgrounds of the Riviera and the Cote d'Azur. And in Holland a hard-driving young businessman founded KLM, a well-managed airline fated for a role far beyond its initial European destinations.

As Europe's airline system slowly took shape, it became apparent that in its fledgling state the industry was economically unviable without additional government support that went well beyond the air mail contracts already provided. European governments took the view that keeping the airlines financially sound was in the national interest and the concept of the national flag carrier was born. Governments greatly increased their financial support for established carriers, smaller airlines were merged into them where appropriate, and the national carriers' financial viability was guaranteed.

Deutsche Lufthansa (initially written as Luft Hansa) and Britain's Imperial Airways were both formed by the merger of a handful of smaller lines by the mid-1920s and KLM and Sabena became established national carriers. By the early 1930s several Swiss carriers merged to form Swiss Air Lines, or Swissair. France's Latécoère had become Aeropostale in 1927 and five years later it merged with Air Union, Air Orient, and CIDNA into Air France. There would be changes and upheavals in the coming years, but Europe's system of national airlines was largely set for the remainder of the twentieth century.

Across the Atlantic, airlines took to wing at a slower pace. America's large area and vast distances made it difficult to provide timely, reliable air service with the fragile, cantankerous machines of the early 1920s. The railroads were king. Fast and efficient, they crisscrossed the nation and carried their passengers coast to coast in three days in grand hotel comfort. Passengers weren't about to desert them in droves for tired surplus World War I sticks-and-canvas airplanes beholden to the weather and unreliable engines.

St. Petersburg-Tampa
AIRBOAT LINE
Fast Passenger and Express Service

SCHEDULE:

Lv. St. Petersburg   10:00 A.M.
Arrive Tampa   10:30 A.M.

Leave Tampa   11:00 A.M.
Ar. St. Petersburg   11:30 A.M.

Lv. St. Petersburg   2:00 P.M.
Arrive Tampa   2:30 P.M.

Leave Tampa   3:00 P.M.
Ar. St. Petersburg   3:30 P.M.

Special Flight Trips

Can be arranged through any of our agents or by communicating directly with the St. Petersburg Hangar. Trips covering any distance over all-water routes and from the waters' surface to several thousand feet high AT PASSENGERS' REQUEST.

A minimum charge of $15 per Special Flight.

Rates: $5.00 Per Trip.   Round Trip $10.   Booking for Passage in Advance.

NOTE—Passengers are allowed a weight of 200 pounds GROSS including hand baggage, excess charged at $5.00 per 100 pounds, minimum charge 25 cents. EXPRESS RATES, for packages, suit cases, mail matter, etc., $5.00 per hundred pounds, minimum charge 25 cents. Express carried from hangar to hangar only, delivery and receipt by shipper.

Tickets on Sale at Hangars or
CITY NEWS STAND
F. C. WEST, Prop.

271 CENTRAL AVENUE   ST. PETERSBURG, FLORIDA

The St. Petersburg-Tampa Airboat Line is generally acknowledged to be the world's first scheduled airline. Launched in 1914, it connected its two namesake towns across Tampa Bay. It saved hours over the journey by sea or land, but with room for only one passenger in its diminutive Benoist flying boats it was more of an exciting experiment than a sustainable airline and operated for only three months before its founders moved on to other adventures.

11

BODENSEE AEROLLOYD

RUND ∗ UND STRECKENFLÜGE AM BODENSEE MIT DORNIER FLUGBOOTEN

An Aerolloyd Dornier Delfin flying boat wings its way across the picturesque Bodensee, which separates Germany and Switzerland. Flying boats were an attractive proposition in the early days of aviation because of the natural landing areas offered by bodies of water, not only for routine operations but also for emergencies. The Delfins took their passengers, most of whom were tourists, on short hops between lakeside destinations.

Air mail was another matter. America's long-standing obsession with speedy communications saw the airplane as the natural successor to train-borne mail. The mail bags took up much less space than passengers, and if the pilot had to bail out of an iced-up airplane above a solid cloud layer the bags could usually be gathered up from wherever they slammed into the ground and sent on their way. By the mid-1920s the U.S. government was willing to dole out massive subsidies to successful bidders for the air mail routes.

A trickle of bold passengers sought out the chance to fly, and, as in Europe several years before, numerous small airlines sprung up throughout the country, many of them competing increasingly for fare-paying customers in addition to the air mail contracts.

America's airlines received a major boost in 1927 when Charles Lindbergh flew nonstop, solo from New York to Paris in thirty hours and the nation went air crazy. Among the early U.S. lines were Robertson Airlines of St. Louis, Missouri, which had counted Charles Lindbergh among its first pilots, and Western Air Express, which tried to make it on passengers alone on its aggressive route network in Southern California and the Southwest. Varney Airlines and Boeing Air Transport plied the air routes of the West Coast and the Northwest, and National Air Transport connected the East Coast with the Midwest. Pitcairn Aviation flew an air mail–only route along the eastern seaboard, and Colonial Air Transport established the first scheduled passenger service between Boston and New York.

By 1929 U.S. airlines had carried 129,000 passengers, the most in the world. Germany was second with 120,000 passengers. The other countries trailed well behind, but Europe as a whole still accounted for twice as many passengers as the United States.

Anthony Fokker's airliners were the most popular passenger liners of the day, but home-grown U.S. competitors were beginning to make their appearance, including two trimotors: the Boeing B-80, and the corrugated metal Ford Trimotor, affectionately dubbed the "Tin Goose."

Transcontinental Air Transport garnered the greatest publicity by establishing America's first transcontinental air service in cooperation with the railroads. TAT's Ford Trimotors flew the passengers by day, and the Pennsylvania Railroad and Santa Fe Railroad took them on two night segments, shaving a full day off the rail-only option. By 1932 the journey was cut to twenty-nine hours and was entirely by air.

America's mosaic of small carriers were characterized by a confusing patchwork of intertwining ownership and faced the same problem as their European counterparts: They were flying in the red. But while the U.S. government understood the importance of the airline industry, it was unwilling to provide direct financial support, unlike the European governments. Instead, it chose to revamp and expand the air mail subsidy to a level that would sustain the strongest companies. To achieve this, it forced a controversial series of mergers around the strongest carriers to create airlines large enough to be economically viable with the support of the proposed subsidies.

So came to prominence America's Big Four domestic carriers that would dominate the U.S. scene for the next half century until deregulation: United Airlines, American Airways, Eastern Air Transport, and Transcontinental and Western Air (immediately shortened in popular parlance to TWA). Pan American Airways, concentrating exclusively on international routes, was scheming to become the nation's sole international flag carrier.

Air transportation benefitted from an epochal advance in 1936 when the twenty-one–passenger, all-metal, twin-engined Douglas DC-3 entered service. Sleek, smooth, streamlined aluminum without a strut in sight, it was the world's first airliner that could be flown at a profit without a mail subsidy. It showed the way and went on to become the industry's dominant airline for years to come.

By the early 1930s the airline industry was firmly entrenched throughout Europe and the United States. The airlines' safety record was beginning to catch up to the railways' and the steadily growing number of airline passengers had taken to bringing their own stylish fur coats, though they still welcomed the occasional foot warmer. Some carriers had even begun to make tentative forays further afield following their nations' worldwide interests, and as the airliners they flew became increasingly more capable and reliable they were poised to encircle the globe.

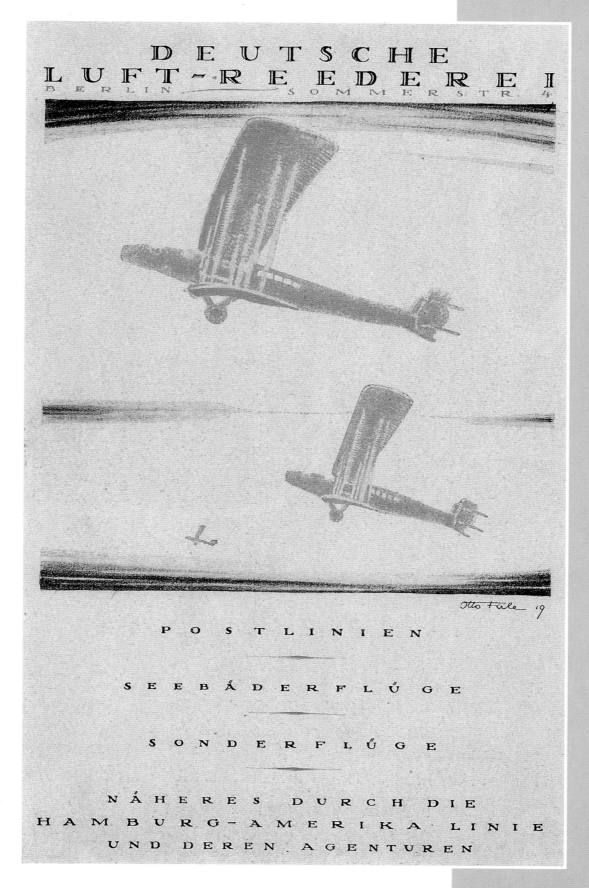

Deutsche Luft Reederei's inaugural flight from Berlin to Weimar in early 1919 was the first scheduled air service in Europe and the beginning of the first sustained airline service in the world. This bold, futuristic poster depicts the German company's three giant Staaken World War I bombers, which were converted to civilian use. Because of chaotic postwar economic conditions and restrictions on the size of German aircraft following World War I, the Staaken bombers were flown only briefly to be replaced by smaller war surplus aircraft.

Pioneering airline passengers were quick to turn necessity into a fashion statement. This chic traveler has her own fur-lined and -trimmed aviator's coat. The foot warmer awaits on board. If she timed her trip right she could look forward to a five-course champagne lunch between London and Paris in the converted Farman Goliath bomber she is about to board. Air Union, founded in 1923, was one of four fledgling French airlines that merged to become Air France in 1933.

The first attempts to establish scheduled passenger air service were made by the Zeppelin airships of DELAG, the German Airship Transport Company, before World War I. While it proved impractical to maintain a reliable schedule with these unwieldy, underpowered, rigid gas bags, which were twice as long as a Boeing 747, they provided immensely popular and surprisingly safe local sightseeing flights. Between 1910 and 1914 they carried more than 10,000 passengers at the cost of one broken leg. Zeppelins would be developed to fly in regular transatlantic passenger service for a decade during the 1920s and 1930s.

The Compagnie des Messageries Aeriennes, a forerunner of Air France, was one of the first French airlines to fly on the prestigious cross-channel Paris–London run in 1919. Its Breguet XIVs, depicted here by Guy Arnoux, were the workhorses of France's early airlines and covered the Paris–London trip in two and a half hours. Arnoux was a well-respected commercial artist. Among the few airline posters he designed are works for Air France.

This fine example of an Art Nouveau poster from 1920 advertises MAEFORT, Hungary's first airline. MAEFORT connected Hungary's capital, Budapest, with several provincial cities, and had a fleet of twenty-two aircraft, including war surplus Fokkers. The venture was promising, but under the harsh terms imposed on the former Austro-Hungarian Empire following World War I, it was forced to shut down after only eighteen months of operations.

Albert Solon's powerful poster shows the Farman F-170 Jabiru airliner, made by Societe Farman, one of France's premier aircraft makers from the earliest days of aviation. It whisked eight passengers toward their destination at 140 miles per hour, an impressive speed for the time. Interiors were carefully crafted to resemble the comfort of competing luxurious train compartments as can be seen in this image (below) of the larger Farman Goliath.

Time is money. The businessman eyeing his watch in this Curtiss Flying Service poster from the 1920s captures the essence of business aviation, which is often invoked today to justify the use and ownership of business aircraft. In reality the dapper businessman may have looked more like the man on the scale in the photograph below. Weighing in to avoid overloading an airplane was a routine practice in the early days. Curtiss was one of America's biggest aircraft and engine makers into the 1950s and operated its own flying service until airline regulations prohibited manufacturers from owning airlines.

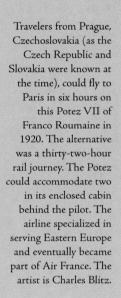

Travelers from Prague, Czechoslovakia (as the Czech Republic and Slovakia were known at the time), could fly to Paris in six hours on this Potez VII of Franco Roumaine in 1920. The alternative was a thirty-two-hour rail journey. The Potez could accommodate two in its enclosed cabin behind the pilot. The airline specialized in serving Eastern Europe and eventually became part of Air France. The artist is Charles Blitz.

Lignes Aériennes G. Latécoère was another forerunner of Air France. Founded in 1919 by Toulouse businessman G. Latécoère, it pioneered the air mail routes to North Africa. Its 850-mile run from Toulouse to Casablanca took thirty hours with ten stops. The swift-looking trimotor pictured in the poster made it to the prototype stage but never flew. The original poster was made of sheet iron, which gave a three-dimensional effect. Latécoère initially operated mostly Breguet XIVs, shown in the photo below over the coastline of southern France.

Dutchman Anthony Fokker's airliners were the most widely used passenger aircraft in the 1920s and early 1930s before being overtaken by the Douglas DC-3. They flew passengers on all continents, even making it to Antarctica with several polar expeditions. The Japan Air Transport Company used both the single-engined and trimotor variants from 1929 between Tokyo, Osaka, and other destinations.

The image of three cranes became the symbol of Deutsche Luft Reederei in 1919 and the crane motif was adopted by Lufthansa upon its formation in 1926. It can be seen to this day on the tail of all Lufthansa aircraft, one of the most enduring emblems of the airline industry.

Latécoère became Aeropostale in 1927 and carried on the serious business of carrying the mail from France all the way down to Dakar, Senegal, in West Africa, and across the Atlantic through South America. This poster evokes the less stressful service of carrying affluent vacationers across southern France to Biarritz, the fashionable south Atlantic resort otherwise accessible by a lengthy train journey.

The Junkers F-13 first took to the air in 1919 and was the world's first all-metal airliner with wings free of unsightly drag-laden struts. It was an extremely rugged airplane, serving worldwide on skis and floats as well as conventional wheels. More than 300 were built and Lufthansa alone had 55 of them at one point.

Colonial Air Transport, one of America's first airlines, made its mark with the first scheduled service between Boston and New York in 1926. By the late 1920s the airline flew the all-metal Ford Trimotor, one of the first U.S. airliners to enjoy wide popularity. The Ford Trimotor, in the accompanying photograph, shown refueling with its engines running belongs to Transcontinental Air Transport, a forerunner of TWA.

A BALATONI LÉGI FORGALOM

ünnepélyes megnyitása

SIÓFOKON

1923. junius 29-én, Péter és Pál napján az AEROEXPRESS R. T. által, Junkers alluminium vizirepülőgépekkel.

Zenés ébresztő, katonazene, térzene.

Körrepülések a Balaton felett

Szépségverseny, tombola, kinófelvétel. Repülőgépmodellek amerikai elárverezése.

Társasvacsora. — Tánc reggelig.

Kedvezményes vasuti utazás oda-vissza, fürdéssel, étkezéssel. Menetrendszerü repülőgépközlekedés a Balaton felett.

ALKALMI JÁRATOK:	
1. **Budapest-Siófok között.**	
3000 méter magasságban.	
3 személy részére, személyenként oda-vissza 80.000 K	
A jegy 24 óráig érvényes, visszautazásra szoló jegy másra átruházható.	
2. **Körrepülés az egész Balaton felett.**	
Indulás és érkezés Siófokra, személyenként 50.000 K	
3. **Kis kör: Siófok, Kenesse, Almádi, Füred, Tihany —— Siófok felett.**	
Személyenként 15.000 K	
Ezenfelül a Balaton bármely pontjára telefonon repülőgép megrendelhető.	

MENETRENDSZERÜ JÁRATOK:

4. Siófok	indul 10ʰ	5. Siófok	indul 17ʰ
Almádi	érkezik 10ʰ 7 / indul 10ʰ 17	Földvár	érkezik 17ʰ 7 / indul 17ʰ 17
Balatonfüred	érkezik 10ʰ 23 / indul 10ʰ 33	Balatonfüred	érkezik 17ʰ 22 / indul 17ʰ 32
Földvár	érkezik 10ʰ 38 / indul 10ʰ 48	Almádi	érkezik 17ʰ 40 / indul 17ʰ 50
Siófok	érkezik 10ʰ 56	Siófok	érkezik 17ʰ 56

Repülőgép rendelhető telefonon is

Budapest		Siófok
Gellértszálló	AEROEXPRESS	Fürdö Igazgatóság.

Molnár-féle Magyar Sajtó Bpest. V. Falk Mikra-utca 11.

The Fokker F-13 on floats in this 1923 poster from Hungary served Lake Balaton, one of Europe's largest lakes. Its longest hop was 10 minutes, its entire route one hour, but it made possible brief excursions that would have required an entire day of surface travel. The F-13 on floats in the photo below served at around the same time 12,000 miles away in the Brazilian wilderness.

AIR UNION

CHARLES PAINE

This Air Union poster by Charles Paine from 1923 captures the airplane's utility on the London–Paris route where train travel could take as long as a day and a half because of the need to cross the Channel by ship. The two-and-a-half-hour crossing by airplane left plenty of time in the day for golf. The airlines competed intensely with fancy meal services on the route, such as this lunch service on a Farman. The intent was to match the dining car services of the cross-channel trains.

PARIS-LONDON-PARIS
BY AIR

LONDRES · PARIS · LYON · MARSEILLE
LYON · GENEVE

Occhipinti

RAPID AZUR

AIR UNION

Air Union expanded quickly to connect northern affluence with the playground of the Cote d'Azur via its gateway, Marseille. The service's name was an inspired choice, the fully enclosed Breguet 280 a small step up from its open cockpit predecessors.

The Handley Page W-10 resembled the 0/400 in which Freya Stark shared the navigator's open cockpit on her first airline flight, but was an entirely new design. This twelve-passenger aircraft flew Imperial Airways' European routes from the mid-1920s. The pictured aircraft evokes Britain's nautical traditions as it flies the flag.

The massive Zeppelin-Staaken four-engined monoplane was another impressive German design of the early 1920s. It made several successful test flights, and the Suddeutsche Lufthansa posters were already printed when the airplane was ordered to be broken up under the conditions imposed by the Allies on Germany in the wake of World War I. Note the many destinations served by the airline.

Air Union's Golden Ray service between Paris and London in the 1920s was one of the earliest prestige runs of the airline industry. The company flew fifteen Farman Goliath bombers converted to civilian use featuring a plush interior and sumptuous dining service. In 1926 an Air Union Goliath broke new ground when it performed the first scheduled night flight between London and Paris.

This poster commemorates an impressive accomplishment by a Lufthansa Junkers F-13 in 1927 demonstrating the reach and safety of air travel. The Junkers had flown 100,000 kilometers, or 60,000 miles, without mishap. Publicizing such performance drew in more passengers and gave them comfort as they climbed up on the corrugated wing to board (below).

An evocative Air Union poster created in 1932 by Maurus entices well-heeled travelers to add hours to their Riviera vacations by opting to fly. The service from the north all the way to Cannes proved to be lucrative for Air Union, and also good publicity as celebrities embraced the thrill of going by air. The airplane is a Breguet 280.

Far from the Riviera, the Ford Trimotor was a solid interim airplane between the wooden-winged Fokkers and the modern Douglas DC-3. All of America's airlines flew them and Ford, who bought William Stout's design and had him put it in production, could have become a bigger player in aviation but eventually decided to stay with its core automobile business.

This Aeropostale image from 1932 accomplishes the period aviation poster's goal to perfection. Who wouldn't want to board an airplane and fly to North Africa upon seeing it? Flying at its best was like this, a stunning sunset over an exotic destination at the end of a tiring day, attracting celebrated pilots such as Jean Mermoz and the writer Antoine St. Exupery.

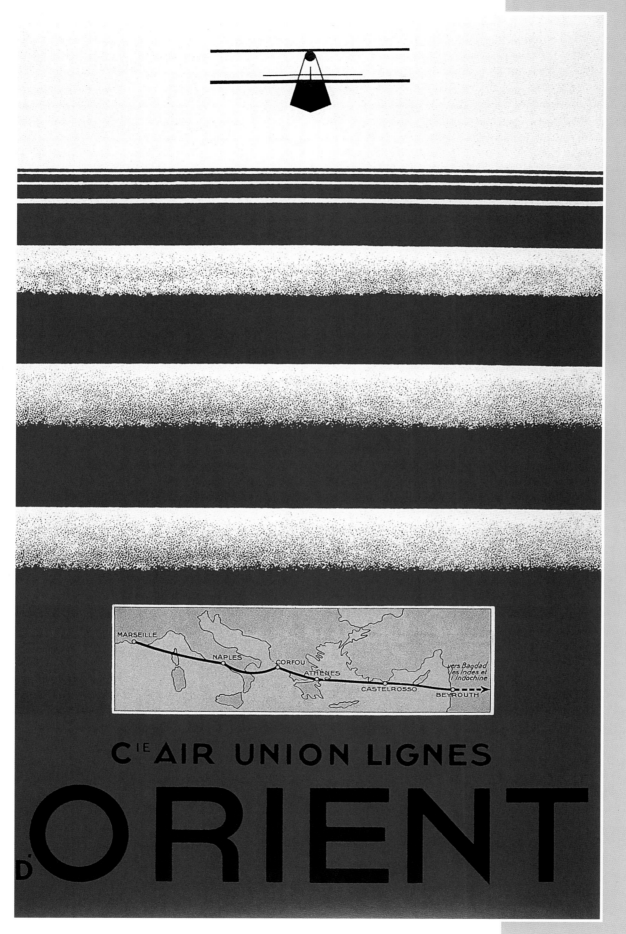

Air Orient, formed in 1930, looked eastward to France's possessions in Indochina as its name implies. Overseas interests were a powerful magnet for the establishment of air services and led to the rapid expansion of routes as more capable aircraft came on stream. Air Union handled the Mediterranean segment of this route with flying boats as far as Beirut, Lebanon, a French protectorate at the time. While Naples, Corfu, and Athens attracted their share of travelers, Castelrosso was primarily a technical stop.

By 1926 Dornier's Wal flying boats were seen in northern European skies with increasing frequency. By 1933 they were flying a unique air mail service across the Atlantic to South America. Using support ships on the high seas they hopped their way across, cutting air mail service to three and a half days from Germany to Buenos Aires, Argentina. In the photograph below a Wal is being hauled aboard a support ship for reprovisioning before being catapulted off its deck to complete its crossing.

Fliegt in die Bäder

This poster celebrates the first crossing of the south Atlantic. It was achieved in 1930 by Aeropostale's Jean Mermoz and his crew in a Latécoère 28 on floats. The trip took twenty-one hours and fifteen minutes from St. Louis de Senegal to Natal, Brazil. Within the next decade such flights became commonplace but continued to retain a fair element of risk, claiming, among others, the life of Jean Mermoz on a subsequent crossing.

Italy played a leading role in the development of commercial aviation that is not always sufficiently acknowledged. Savoia Marchetti landplanes ranged across the continent and the company's double-fuselaged flying boats covered the Mediterranean. The flying boats gained international attention in 1933 when General Italo Balbo led a twenty-five-strong formation across the Atlantic to the Chicago World Fair.

Once commercial airline services became established, could the discount fare be far behind? As early as 1926 Lufthansa was offering a 20-percent discount on the published price of round-trip air fares. The silhouette represents the first of the Junkers trimotors, the JU-31. The airport bus meeting passengers (in the photograph below) advertises flights to twenty-eight of Lufthansa's many destinations, including Budapest, Moscow, Copenhagen, and Zurich.

Fur Coats and Foot Warmers 41

By 1930 London society could buzz about the continent as never before on a number of European airlines. A growing variety of trimotors offered redundancy in case of engine failure and provided the performance to haul their passengers in style. In the photograph below Lufthansa passengers on a Junkers 31 enjoy another fine dining experience to distract them from the noise, vibration, and turbulence characteristic of most journeys by air. The poster artist is Otto Arpke.

DEUTSCHE LUFT HANSA

GERMAN AIRWAYS

DAILY CONNECTIONS EXCEPT SUNDAYS TO AND FROM
AMSTERDAM · BERLIN · BREMEN · COLOGNE DORTMUND · DÜSSELDORF · ESSEN · FRANCFORT HALLE/LEIPZIG · HAMBURG · HANNOVER MOSCOW · MUNICH

This Northwest Airlines poster is one of the most innovative examples of airline advertising during the 1930s. It dispels any concern about the safety of flight as the little girl tells the chick that flying is as easy as Northwest's perky Lockheed Electra makes it look. The Electra (seen in the accompanying photograph) was smaller than the DC-3 but technologically as advanced. It was popular on thinly traveled routes throughout the world. The artist is George Rupp.

This well-known Aeropostale poster represents the era of the 1920s when aircraft derived from World War I designs were establishing a viable niche for commercial aviation in the world's transportation system. Within a decade they were made obsolete by the Douglas DC-3 (opposite page), a rate of progress akin to the development of the computer industry at the end of the twentieth century.

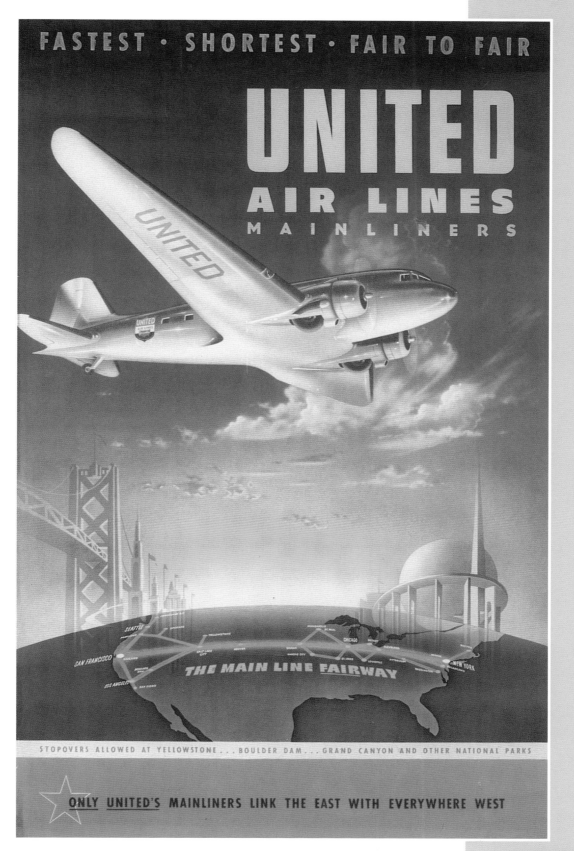

By 1936 the era of the fur coat and the foot warmer was consigned to memory by the appearance of the Douglas DC-3. The first to be able to make a profit without air mail subsidies, it ushered in the era of the modern propliner and quickly became the most popular airliner in the world.

GOING GLOBAL

When H. R. Ekins of the *Scripps Howard Journal* alighted from a TWA flight at Newark, New Jersey, in late 1936 he secured a place in the annals of air travel. He had become the first person ever to complete a round-the-world trip by air as a fare-paying passenger on scheduled flights readily available to anyone willing to buy a ticket.

On his marathon circular journey Ekins relied on every mode of commercial air transport in service in the 1930s. He set off in the grandest style available to air travelers, from Lakehurst, New Jersey, onboard the airship *Hindenburg* bound for Frankfurt, Germany. From there he put himself in the care of KLM Royal Dutch Airlines and made his way to Athens for a bit of classic tourism, and then on to Batavia, Indonesia, in one of the revolutionary Douglas airliners the progressive airline had recently acquired. KLM's Far Eastern subsidiary, KNILM, got him to Manila in a reliable old Fokker trimotor made obsolete by the DC-3.

In Manila Ekins boarded one of Pan American's four-engined Martin M-130 flying boats, the *Hawaii Clipper*, to tackle the most challenging air route of the time: the vast, monotonous trek across the Pacific to California. There was little margin for error and less hope for being found and rescued in case of an emergency water landing hundreds of miles from one of Pan Am's tiny island bases. But the trip went off without a hitch with a welcome break from the tedium of long-distance flying in Honolulu, Hawaii, before embarking on the longest segment, the 2,400-mile nonstop overnight leg to San Francisco. Safely beyond the Golden Gate Bridge, it was on to the landplanes of United and TWA with

a light heart for an uneventful transcontinental flight home to New York.

The airlines were shrinking the globe, according to the period cliché, and Ekins' trip proved it, although it could have ended differently. Within a year the *Hindenburg* burned on arrival at Lakehurst, putting an end to airship travel, and the *Hawaii Clipper* disappeared without a trace between Guam and Manila, wiping out a third of Pan American's transpacific M-130 fleet. But such setbacks were considered the cost of progress, to be taken in stride. On balance the headlines had more to celebrate than mourn, and steadfastly the airlines spun their web of routes to the farthest reaches of the globe.

Airline expansion was driven by the rapid advance of aviation technology. Airliners were becoming bigger, faster, more comfortable, and more reliable. Large, plush flying boats found natural airports in sheltered ocean bays, and on lakes and rivers, even in the wildest jungles of the world, and accounted for a significant share of long-distance airline service. For a time the giant airships had a glamorous role. Boeing built the first pressurized airliner, the four-engined Stratoliner, and Douglas set the standard with the DC-3. Advances in instrument flying and navigation, particularly guidance by radio beam, made the skies safer and schedules easier to maintain.

While the technology was increasingly available by the 1930s to crisscross the world on schedule, profits remained elusive until the DC-3 began to make its mark toward the end of the decade. The answer was once again air mail, the need for fast communication with far-flung business interests and colonial possessions. Government mail contracts and, in most instances, direct support in the name of national interest paid for going global in the

WINGS TO GUATEMALA

IT'S A SMALL WORLD BY
Pan American World Airways
The System of the Flying Clippers

Guatemala was one of Pan American's many Central American stops served by its Douglas airliners in the second half of the 1930s. This poster by P. G. Lawler is one of a series dating from 1938 that emphasized destination over comforts of the aircraft or seeking to allay safety fears. As air travel became more accepted, advertisers' attention turned to portraying the promise of quick access to exotic lands.

1930s. The groundwork had been laid during the 1920s with a series of military and civilian survey flights that led first to regular air mail service followed by the carriage of passengers.

The national airlines of countries with large-scale overseas interests took the lead in opening up the airways between distant continents. Within a decade after their first tentative inter-European forays, three airlines linked the Far East with Europe. KLM operated between Holland and Indonesia, Air France flew between France and Indochina, and Imperial Airways connected Britain with India and Singapore, from where Australia's Quantas Empire Airways continued on down under as far as Sydney and Melbourne.

Routes to eastern and southern Africa were established equally swiftly by Imperial Airways, which spanned the continent from Capetown, South Africa, all the way to Egypt,

A light twin-engined aircraft of Air Afrique
swoops low over the indigenous population of
Bamako, Mali, in this idealized view of the
march of progress. All the big airlines used
smaller craft on local feeder networks that fed
their intercontinental flights.

times the range of their nearest competitor. They opened routes from the U.S. West Coast to Hawaii and on to the Philippines, Hong Kong, China, and even New Zealand. Only another policy conflict with imperial Britain barred them from Australia.

As the 1930s were drawing to a close Pan American turned its attention back to the Atlantic and launched service from New York to Foynes, Ireland, and via the Azores and Lisbon, Portugal, to Marseilles, France. After the airline's experience in the Pacific it was little more than a hop across a pond for its new behemoth Boeing flying boats, the 747s of their age.

Even Germany, shorn of its colonies after World War I, but maintaining the most sophisticated airline services in Europe, got to play an important global role. Lufthansa subsidiaries in partnership with local interests helped Aeroflot establish scheduled air service throughout the Soviet Union, and developed commercial aviation in China, even operating a flight to Kabul in neighboring Afghanistan. German airlines were also prominent throughout South America, encouraged by a vibrant German expatriate community. Lufthansa established a unique transatlantic air mail service to South America with Dornier Wal flying boats that landed alongside a chain of stationary service ships to refuel enroute.

During the late 1920s and 1930s Germany gave the world the Zeppelin airship, a mode of global air travel so luxurious with its lounges, dining rooms, promenade walkways, and private cabins, that it is unlikely to be ever matched in scheduled air service. For almost a decade the *Graf Zeppelin* made routine crossings of the Atlantic to North and South America, joined later by the *Hindenburg*, an even bigger and more opulent leviathan. They easily attracted ocean liner passengers who could make the crossing in accustomed comfort in half the time. But the *Hindenburg's* fiery demise at Lakehurst, New Jersey, in 1937 ended their era.

In addition to their rivalry with the railways, the airliners were also competing with boats for passengers, slashing the time it took to complete long-distance journeys. By 1936 Imperial Airways had cut the trip from Britain

where it connected with its other services to London. Air France steadily expanded its inherited North African and French West African presence, and the Belgian national airline, Sabena, linked Brussels with the Belgian Congo and central Africa.

Air France also connected Europe, Africa, and Latin America by building on Aeropostale's gutsy South American air mail network and the route across the southern Atlantic between Dakar, Senegal, and Natal, Brazil, pioneered by the legendary pilot Jean Mermoz and his colleagues.

By the early 1930s Pan American Airways was expanding at an aggressive pace that would eventually make it the world's dominant international airline. It blanketed Central and South America with a network of air routes to serve the considerable business interests of U.S. multinational companies in the Southern Hemisphere with a mixed fleet of flying boats and landplanes. When its plans to go transatlantic were delayed by a squabble with the British over route rights it turned its attention westward and realized its greatest accomplishment of the 1930s by conquering the Pacific. Its flying boats, designed especially for the task, had four to India from three weeks by boat to as little as three days by air. But that didn't necessarily mean an instant flood of passengers to the Imperial ticket offices. The civil servants and business people working abroad who accounted for the majority of travelers had a lifestyle to match the leisurely pace of going by sea. They remained in their postings for years before going on home leave for as long as six months, and many of them welcomed the familiar comfort of an unhurried cruise each way as part of their vacation.

The airlines won converts by redefining the prevailing lifestyle. It suddenly became possible to go home for little more than the price of first-class boat passage on the annual short leaves of a few weeks that had hitherto been spent locally. Children, who had been permanently shipped to boarding school at an early age, could join their parents for the summer and even the Christmas holidays. Government officials and company executives on urgent business saw their productivity soar. And millionaire tourists and big-game hunters sped by air to reach their destinations more quickly after years of going by boat.

Competing with the sumptuous service to be found on many passenger ships and charging rates in line with the cost of shipboard journeys, the airlines could not rely on their speed advantage alone to win customers. The comfort and safety of their passengers were equally important. Imperial Airways even sacrificed speed on some of their aircraft types by accepting a bulky fuselage for the sake of a roomier passenger cabin. Most airlines on long-distance overland routes flew only during the day to keep navigation simpler and avoid the risk of emergency landings in darkness over some of the world's most inhospitable terrain. Passengers were put up in first-class hotels overnight and, whenever possible, daytime meals were served in similar surroundings on the ground during interim stops.

Still, the typical long-distance passenger was in for a long, exhausting day. The wakeup call with morning tea could come as early as 4:30 A.M. with an hour to get ready before the limousine left for the airport or the flying boat jetty. Dawn-to-dusk flying was typical with enroute stops every 500 miles or so. In spite of the companies' best efforts, the day's unpressurized airliners were noisy, drafty, lumbering machines. They wallowed around uncomfortably in thermal turbulence, commonly inducing air sickness, and could give a terrifying ride through violent weather. Dinner at a five-star hotel may not have been all that appealing at the end of a long flying day, especially when passengers noted the hour of the following morning's wakeup call. Still, it was glamorous, part of the adventure of slashing the time to reach destinations profusely more exotic than any today, in a world that was larger, less worldly, and far less homogenous than ours.

Across the Pacific, Pan American had to create an entire infrastructure to support its flights. Midway, Wake, and Guam, strategically located drops in the ocean 1,200 to 1,600 miles apart, were chosen to serve as overnight stops for the airline's flying boats. Safe landing channels had to be established, and maintenance facilities, fuel depots, and comfortable transit hotels that maintained standards to which Pan Am's passengers were accustomed had to be built. Long-range radio beacons pioneered by the company had to be installed to enable the flying boats to find the islands. On such long, nonstop routes Pan American couldn't afford to fly only by day. Some segments were flown at night, but departures and arrivals were always timed to take place in daylight.

When a flying boat took off on a transpacific sector the sense of distance and exposure were greater than on the land routes. There was no interim stop in a few hours for a good stretch and a leisurely meal in a plush restaurant. Passengers were confined onboard for ten to eighteen hours at a time with nothing but water below in an aircraft far less reliable than a modern jet. Spacious seating, a lounge and dining room, sleeping berths for the overnight flights, and an onboard service of impeccably high standards compensated for the long hours aloft. And the enticing tropics or sophisticated California awaited at journey's end.

As the 1930s drew to a close there were no important destinations left in the world where the airlines didn't go. They proved that air travel could be consistent, reliable, and global. But flying was still a rich person's game. Airliners rarely carried more than a dozen passengers per flight on the long-distance routes, and in many parts of the world service was sparse. Flying boats still reigned within their domain, but their days were numbered. The faster, more capable landplanes that would replace them, such as the Douglas DC-4 and the Lockheed Constellation, were already on the drawing board even before World War II broke out. And the war would give commercial aviation such a massive technical boost that it would turn air travel from the rarefied privilege of the few into the most popular form of mass transportation.

Pan American was America's most exotic airline during the 1930s. Its relentless quest to reach the farthest corners of the globe thrilled the popular imagination in a way that is difficult to grasp today. Pan American rightly viewed Latin America as its own back yard, and Rio de Janeiro was its most glittering destination. Here a twenty-four-passenger Sikorsky S-42 flying boat arrives over Sugarloaf Mountain after a long series of hops down the coast from Miami, Florida. The artist is P. G. Lawler.

FLYING DOWN TO RIO

IT'S A SMALL WORLD BY

PAN AMERICAN AIRWAYS

Holland's KLM used the Flying Dutchman theme for decades in its advertising posters. The slogan "legend becomes fact" was featured on most variations. Founded in 1919, KLM is one of the world's oldest airlines. In 1929 it launched its first long-range route from Amsterdam to Dutch-controlled Indonesia and went on to become a premier global airline. The aircraft featured here is a fifteen-passenger Fokker F-VIII, also shown below at Schiphol, Amsterdam, being readied for departure. The poster is one of a series done by Jan Wijga.

Air Afrique was formed to serve France's central and West African colonies. Many a pith helmeted government official followed the long route depicted on the map in the young man's hand to an assignment that could last for years. When the colonies achieved independence Air Afrique was reformed as a consortium airline owned by several countries in the region with the help of Air France and UAT. It ceased operations in 2002. The artist is Roquin.

Imperial Airways, founded in 1924 through a government consolidation of several smaller British airlines, linked London with the remotest outposts of the British Empire. Its prestige route was its Indian service, flown by a mixed fleet of flying boats and landplanes. The C-Class Calcutta boat pictured below flew the long overwater leg across the Mediterranean from Italy to Egypt.

Pan American's routes enveloped South America like the proverbial spider web by the 1930s. The 2,000-mile-long Andes mountain range could unleash capricious weather in a flash even on the less-challenging coastal routes. Venturing into its passes could ruffle the nerves of veteran pilots flying the day's most modern airliner, the DC-2. Along the west coast of South America, Pan American operated chiefly through Pan American Grace Airways (PANAGRA), a joint venture owned in equal measure by Pan Am and the W. R. Grace Company, one of the most influential U.S. multinationals in the region.

A Handley Page HP-42 approaches journey's end in the early 1930s. The trip from London took a week, three times faster than going by boat. Passengers arrived in Egypt from Italy in flying boats and boarded the HP-42s for points further east. The HP-42s also flew European routes, operating from Croydon, London's main airport before World War II.

Germany's giant Zeppelin airships provided the most luxurious transoceanic air services ever. Following its highly publicized round-the-world trip in 1928 the *Graf Zeppelin* entered scheduled transatlantic service to North and South America. In 1936 it was joined by the *Hindenburg*, shown here, which made the crossing from Germany to New York in only two days. The *Hindenburg's* passengers enjoyed cocktails on the viewing platform before taking their seats in the dining room. After dinner they danced to the strains of a baby grand piano before retiring to private cabins for the night. The *Hindenburg's* fiery end at Lakehurst, New Jersey, in 1937 brought the airship era to a close. The artist is Anton.

IN 2 DAYS ACROSS THE ATLANTIC
DEUTSCHE ZEPPELIN-REEDEREI
HAMBURG-AMERIKA LINIE

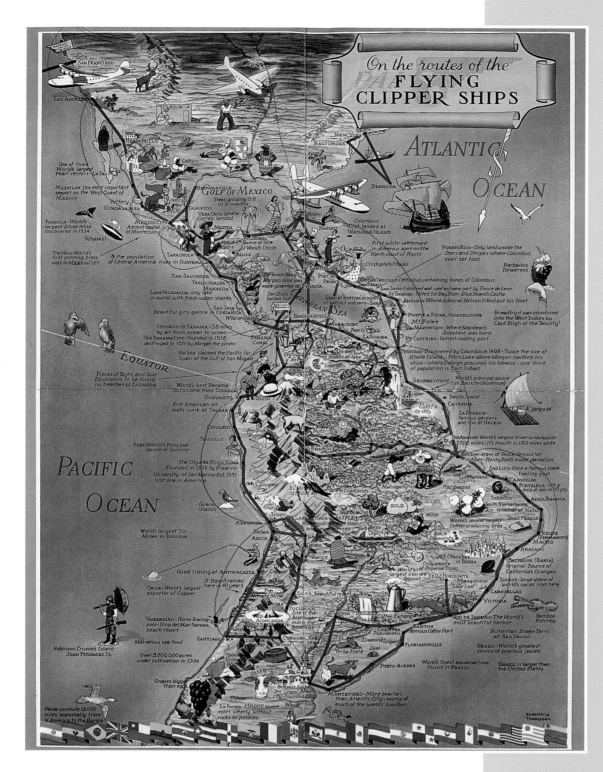

This colorful Pan American route map from the late 1930s helped pass the time during the long, bumpy hours aloft and provided amusing tidbits of information about the region. The thin red line on the map was drawn by its original owner, tracing an actual journey, much of it flown in an S-40 flying boat like the one shown in the accompanying photograph. It reveals that not all flights stopped at all locations.

A rare set of lithographs features the world's first pressurized airliner, the four-engined Boeing 307 Stratoliner, which entered service in 1940. Transcontinental and Western Air, which at the time was a domestic airline, flew five Stratoliners between the east and west coasts of the United States. Pan American had six, based in South America. While its pressurization was a great success, enabling it to cruise above 20,000 feet to avoid most of the bad weather, the Stratoliner's range fell short of expectations. It required two stops to cross the United States, the same as the more profitable and equally fast DC-3.

Created in 1932, this is a rare airline poster by Cassandre, the master of Art Deco advertising. He is using an innovative montage of art and photography to link the Eiffel Tower and the temples of Indochina *par avion*. While passenger services captured all the attention, it was air mail that paid the way. Cassandre (also known as Adolphe Mouron) is best known for his dramatic air-brush work portraying railroad steam engines and transatlantic ships.

Deutsche Luft Hansa

The diesel-powered, thirty-four-seat Junkers G-38, introduced by Lufthansa in 1931, was one of Junkers' more outlandish creations and one of the early four-engined airliners. Three passengers could sit in each massive wing root facing forward and enjoying the view through panoramic windows. Lufthansa operated only two G-38s, but they were in service throughout Europe for years and drew a crowd wherever they went.

K. SIEGWARDT

By the early 1930s the Paris–London route was cut to an hour and a half, not much more than the trip by jet in today's crowded skies. The trimotor flying in the Eiffel Tower's shadow is a French Wibault Penhoet 28. With its contemporaries it made possible day trips between the two capitals. Flying over for lunch became a status trip for the "in crowd."

On Imperial Airways' comfort routes, gentlemen's favorite club chairs have acquired wings according to this pitch. Airlines worked hard to overcome public unease not only about safety, but also the perception of a cold, noisy, cramped flight in flimsy wicker chairs in comparison to the plush comforts of a private overnight compartment on a slower, if safer, train.

Over Sea

ONLY "VIA PAN AMERICAN" CAN YOU TRAVEL ABOARD THE FAMOUS FLEET OF

THE FLYING CLIPPER SHIPS

THE WORLD'S FINEST AIRCRAFT

Over Land

Cutaways were popular poster material to publicize the inner comforts of the modern airliner. Here Pan American promotes its latest acquisitions, the Sikorsky S-42 flying boat, which flew the transpacific survey flights in addition to serving South America, and the DC-3, which became a mainstay of the Latin American land routes.

KLM was one of the first airliners to introduce the Douglas DC-2 in 1934 and its successor, the DC-3, in 1936. A KLM DC-2 took part in the Mac Robertson air race from England to Australia in 1934, maintaining its normal schedule along the way and finishing second behind a single-seat British racing airplane built especially for the occasion. The Douglas airliners spelled the end of Anthony Fokker's design efforts, prompting him to become the European distributor for Douglas in the few years left before World War II destroyed any European hopes of developing a competitive alternative to the DC-3. The artist is Jan Wijga.

By 1939 the Savoia Marchetti SM-83 trimotors of Italy's Ala Littoria had launched scheduled service to South America across the south Atlantic. Argentina's large Italian community was the driving force behind the flights, but the outbreak of World War II shut down the short-lived service. A military version of the SM-83 was Italy's principal bomber at the time. The artist is Bonacini.

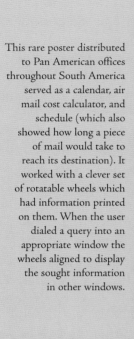

This rare poster distributed to Pan American offices throughout South America served as a calendar, air mail cost calculator, and schedule (which also showed how long a piece of mail would take to reach its destination). It worked with a clever set of rotatable wheels which had information printed on them. When the user dialed a query into an appropriate window the wheels aligned to display the sought information in other windows.

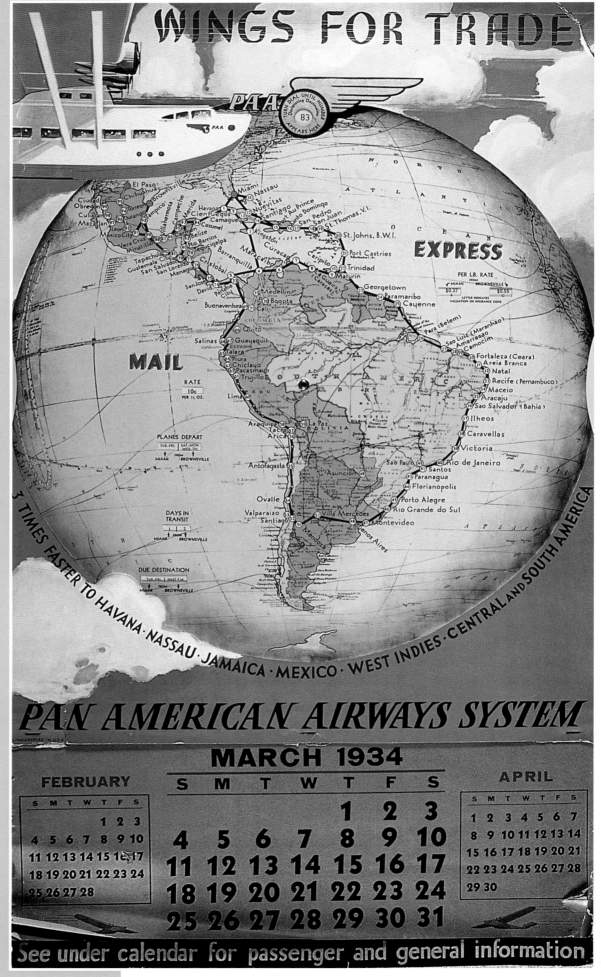

By 1937 Air France ranged throughout Europe, provided regular service to Asia and Africa, and also flew local routes in South America. The figures in local costume around the Bloch 120 illustrate the airline's reach and also show the liberties the companies took to subtly exaggerate their capabilities. The Native American figure is misleading because Air France did not fly to North America at the time. It was included under the pretext of future services vaguely promised to be imminent. The artist is P. Chanove.

Here is another poster in
P. G. Lawler's series for
Pan American featuring
Latin American destinations.
Ecuador was served by
PANAGRA, Pan Am's joint
venture with the W. R. Grace
Company. The relationship
between the two companies
turned acrimonious because
Pan American blocked every
W. R. Grace effort to expand
PANAGRA's routes northward
to the United States.

DEUTSCHE LUFTHANSA
AUCH IM WINTER

The Lufthansa Junkers JU-52 trimotor over this frigid scene makes the point that winter is no obstacle for the airline. Lufthansa was a pioneer in expanding technical capabilities to provide reliable scheduled air service in all but the most extreme conditions. The airline did landmark work in night flying, instrument flying, and winter operations. The seventeen-seat JU-52, which first flew in 1930, is viewed as Europe's equivalent to the DC-3, especially because of the great weight it could lift for its size. Lufthansa even flew them into Kabul, Afghanistan, under the auspices of Eurasia Aviation, a little-known Far Eastern subsidiary that had an extensive network centered on China.

The airplane's ability to bridge cultures practically instantly was one of its most compelling aspects for many early airline passengers. This poster, created in 1933 by Paul Colin, expresses the new closeness created by the airplane between Europe and the Far East. Later in 1933 Air Orient was one of four airlines that merged to form Air France. The winged seahorse in the lower right corner became Air France's trademark symbol.

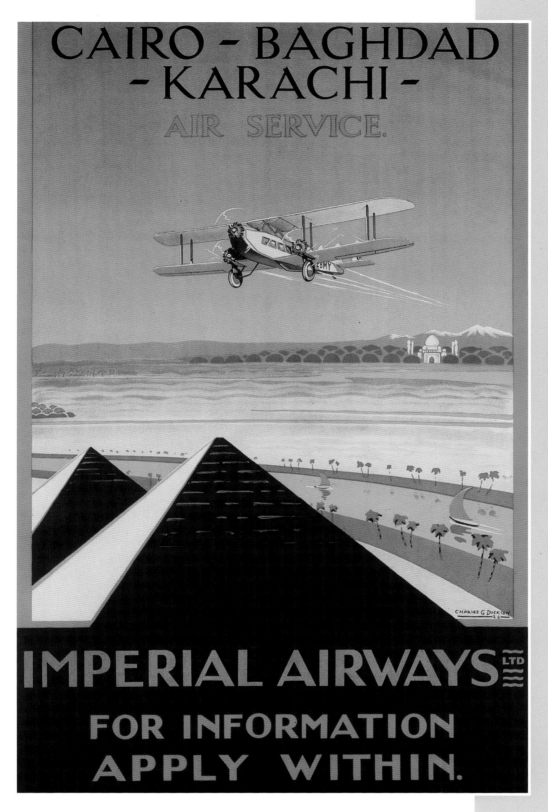

Imperial Airways'
Karachi–Baghdad–Cairo route,
established in 1926, acquired and
consolidated air mail route segments
established by the Royal Air Force
in the Middle East and the Indian
subcontinent. The de Havilland
DH 66 Hercules launched Imperial
Airways' service between India and
Egypt, carrying primarily cargo
and mail, but with room for eight
passengers. They navigated the
featureless Middle Eastern desert
by following an oil-sprinkled dirt
road hacked out between their
destinations to service emergency
landing fields along the way.
The artist is Charles Dickson.

Introduced in 1936, Air France's Dewoitine D338s could carry up to twenty-two passengers, but flew with only six on board on its service between France and Indochina. The low number of passengers allowed for more fuel to extend the airplane's range and left plenty of room for sleeping berths and the ever important air mail sacks. Although fast for its time, it was no match for KLM's DC-3s on the Far Eastern run.

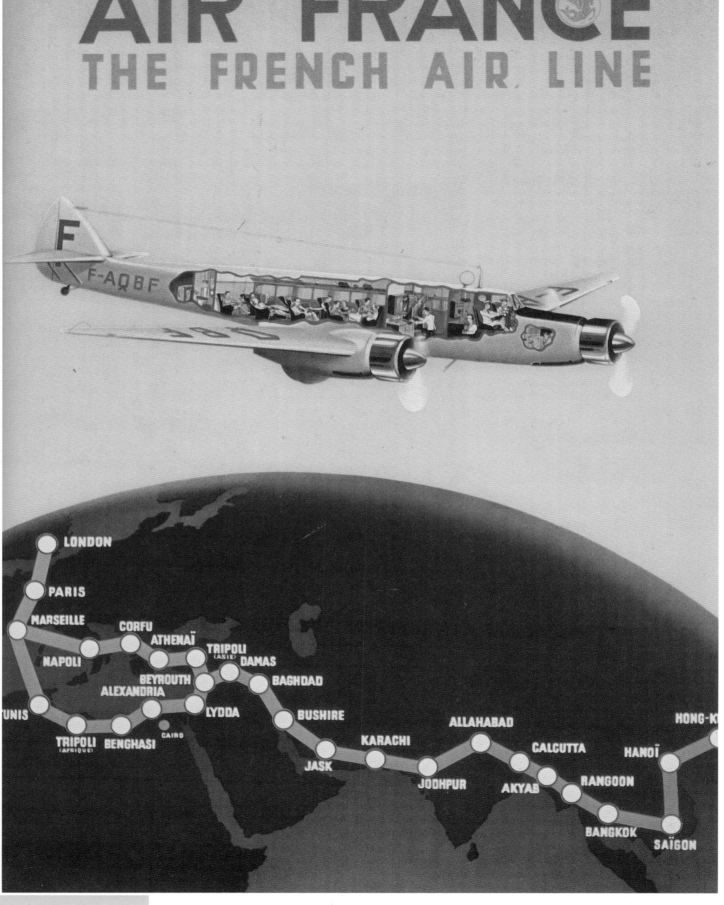

IMPERIAL AIRWAYS

FOR LONGER LEAVE IN
ENGLAND
FLY HOME
INCLUSIVE FARES
'NO EXTRAS'

LEE-ELLIOTT

This 1935 poster by T. Lee-Elliot entices English expatriates working in Africa to fly to Britain on Imperial Airways so that they could spend more time at home instead of enroute. As air travel became more affordable it changed travel patterns. Europeans working in Asia and Africa were able to fly home on leave more frequently instead of taking short breaks locally and going home only once every five or six years for several months. Note the Speedbird symbol, overprinted on the poster, which remained in use long after the airline was restructured into British Overseas Airways Corporation (BOAC). The photograph below shows a Handley Page HP-42 preparing to leave Khartoum, Sudan, a key stop on the African network.

Lucien Boucher's coveted map reveals the extent of Air France's network by 1937. It was a system eighteen years in the making, with roots in Cie. Messageries Aeriennes' first tentative runs to London, Latécoère's air mail routes to North and West Africa extended by Aeropostale across the Atlantic to South America, and Air Orient's trailblazing service to Indochina. The relatively sparse service to France's holdings in Africa hides the fact that they were served primarily by Air Afrique.

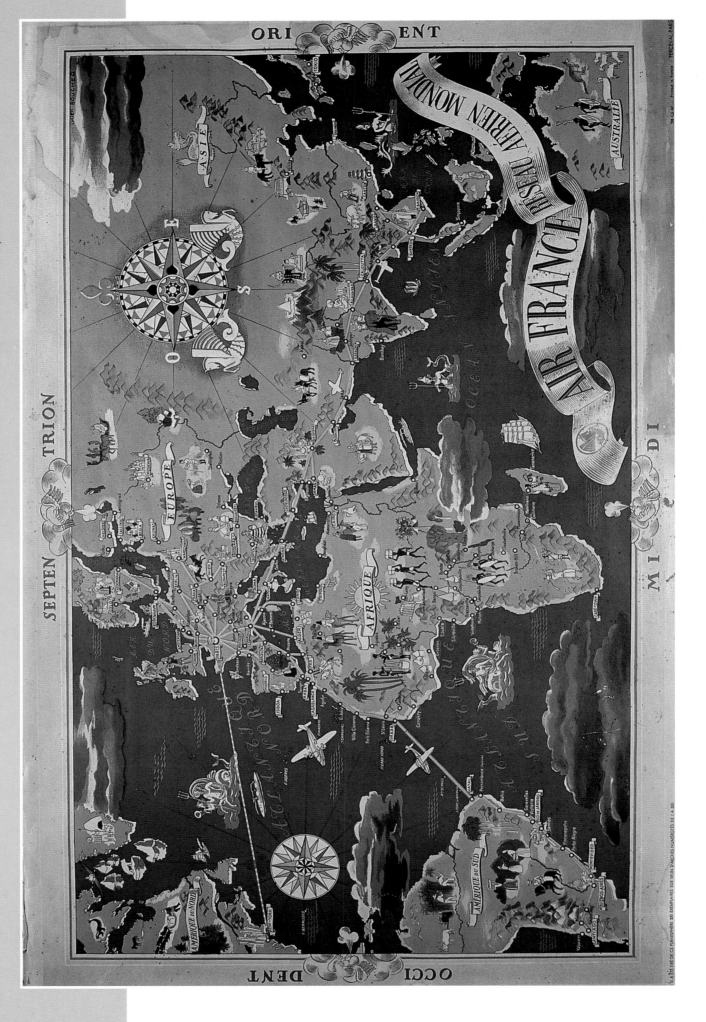

Switzerland had been a popular destination for Britons ever since the Victorians discovered the Alps, and Imperial Airways' Short Scyllas increased the time holiday makers had to ramble among the peaks. The Scylla's designers deliberately sacrificed speed for passenger comfort by giving it a passenger cabin as wide as a railroad car, which created a lot of drag.

The Belgian airline Sabena was another important long-range player that expanded as quickly as technology allowed, motivated by Belgium's links to its African colony, the Belgian Congo. Sabena's predecessors had established a local air mail network in the Congo in the 1920s, and the airline launched its Brussels-Leopoldville service in 1929 with Fokker F-VII trimotors. Here one of Sabena's seventeen-seat Savoia Marchetti SM-73s crosses the Sahara on its way to the Congo in 1936.

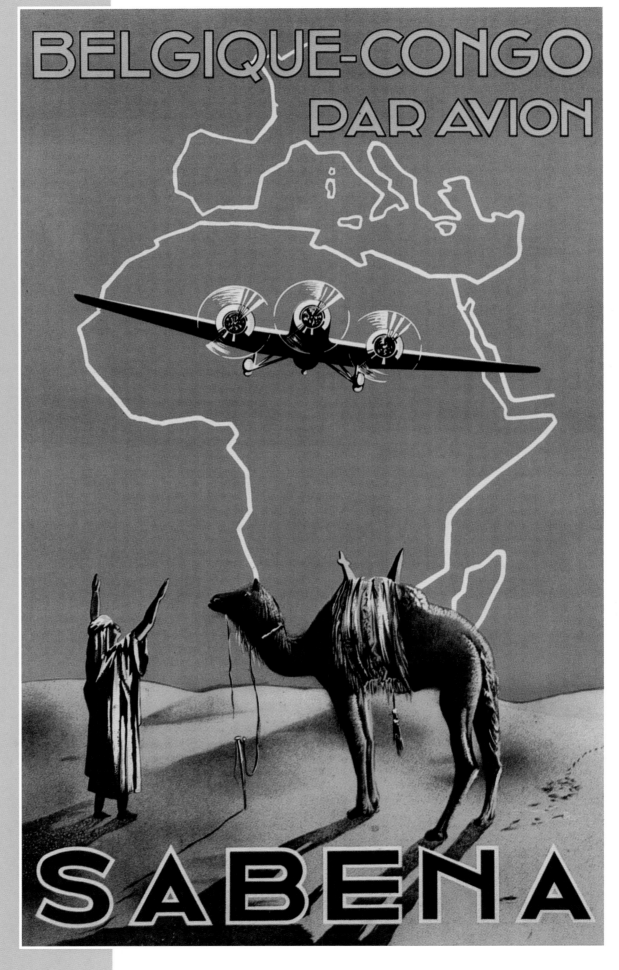

Luftreisen!

– aber wie?

BERLIN

DEUTSCHE LUFTHANSA

SIEGWARD

A Lufthansa Heinkel 111 boards its stylish passengers in 1936. Influenced by German civil aviation's early links to the great German shipping lines, Lufthansa's staff sported nautical dress at the time. Sleek, aerodynamic machines, the Heinkels were fast but a bit cramped for airline service. The military version became Germany's most important bomber in World War II, retracing in massive formations many of the routes flown by Lufthansa's Heinkels in happier times.

Swiss Air Lines, or Swissair, was one of the first customers for the Douglas DC-2, acquiring four of them in 1935. The company was especially attracted by the DC-2's excellent climb performance even with one engine out, a particularly useful characteristic around the Alps. They mostly flew the London–Zurich route with a stop in Basle. Swissair also acquired the DC-3 as soon as it became available.

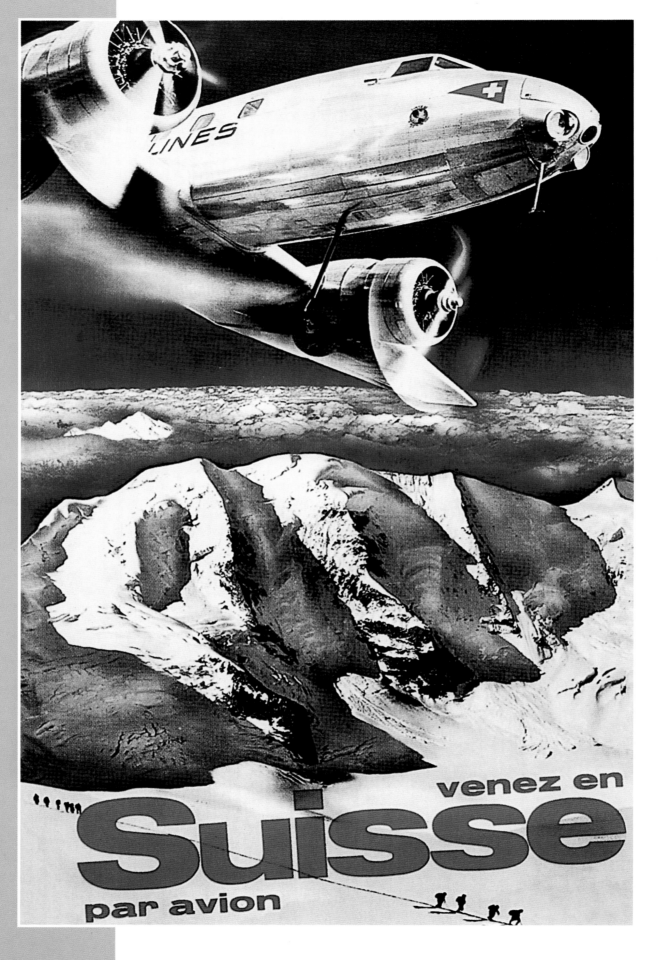

An Imperial Airways Scylla cuts an imperial sight on arrival at London's Croydon Airport. Britain's flag carrier went to especially great lengths to treat its passengers with great pomp and circumstance. In the adjoining photograph passengers are boarding Imperial's prestigious Silver Wing service to Paris flown in this instance by the Scylla's competitor, the HP-42.

IMPERIAL AIRWAYS
AND ASSOCIATED COMPANIES
EUROPE · AFRICA · INDIA · CHINA · AUSTRALIA

One of the most coveted airline posters celebrates the arrival in Honolulu from San Francisco of Pan American's most advanced, largest, and last flying boat, the Boeing 314. Faster, pressurized landplanes would soon make it obsolete, but the Boeing 314 briefly took transoceanic flying to a new level of luxury with its dining lounge, sleeping berths for everyone, and aft honeymoon suite. It was a welcome addition to Pan American's stretched transpacific fleet, which was struggling to maintain scheduled service all the way to Hong Kong with a handful of earlier flying boats. The script usually found on these posters has been cropped out of this image.

The four-engined de Havilland DH 86 of Quantas Empire Airways carried passengers across Australia and Indonesia on the London–Sydney route jointly operated with Imperial Airways. Imperial flew as far as Singapore, where passengers switched to Quantas. This commemorative poster issued by Quantas shows the DH 86 arriving at one of the many typical jungle outposts, which provided such a contrast with deplaning at Croydon or Le Bourget. Everyone who is anyone at the outpost has turned out for the day's most exciting event.

Imperial Airways' Empire flying boats were the most luxurious and capable flown by the airline. Introduced in 1937, they flew all the long-range routes to India, Australia, and Africa from their home port of Southampton, which they shared with the grand ocean liners. Long after the flying boats were gone, even the most jaded travelers held fond memories of being coddled in their richly upholstered compartments and landing at such exotic spots as Victoria Falls, the Nile, and Bombay harbor for sumptuous meals and overnight stays in grand hotels. The Canopus was the first of Imperial Airways' twenty-eight Empire-class boats. Its sister ship, the Corsair, pictured here on the Nile at Cairo, later made a crash landing on a tributary of the Congo with all hands saved. The artist is A. Brenet.

FLY TO SOUTH SEA ISLES

P. G. Lawler's interpretation of Pacific bliss Pan American style is one of the best-known aviation posters of the 1930s. It shows a Boeing 314 landing in the bay at Pago Pago, the most challenging seaplane base in Pan American's Pacific network. Pan American flew to Pago Pago and on to New Zealand only intermittently at this time. Thwarted by British regulators from access to the bigger market of Australia, the company found the New Zealand route uneconomical and gave priority to serving the Philippines and China. Its twelve-to-eighteen-hour nonstop legs across the featureless Pacific were an unparalleled achievement of aviation technology and navigation.

Via PAN AMERICAN

A popular fold-out poster depicts Imperial Airways' most widely used aircraft in the late 1930s. It is interesting to browse the airplanes' performance figures. In 1937 Imperial Airways carried 76,000 passengers 6,000,000 miles worldwide, a commendable feat from one airline of an industry that didn't even exist two decades before.

By 1941, as America was about to become embroiled in World War II, Pan American had flown farther than any other airline. Entrenched in Latin America, it had also conquered the Pacific and was flying to Europe and Africa. Only government route restrictions kept it from establishing a round-the-world service. The airlines had conquered the globe, but as events would soon show, their collective achievements in the 1920s and 1930s amounted to only the first tentative steps of an infant compared to what was about to come.

PROPLINER SPLENDOR

I n the late afternoon on October 24, 1945, a Douglas DC-4 took off from Hanscom Field in the western suburbs of Boston, Massachusetts, and set course for London, England. The four-engined propliner seemed huge to the reporters present, whose yardstick for the modern airliner was the twin-engined DC-3. Its forty-four-seat cabin could carry over twice the number of passengers as the DC-3. Its 2,000-mile range could take it twice as far, and its 215-mile-per-hour cruise speed was 35 miles per hour faster. Much was made by the press of the New England clam chowder, the lobster thermidor, and the Indian pudding with ice cream served for dinner on board before the passengers settled in for the long night ahead, disrupted by refueling stops in Gander, Newfoundland, and Keflavik, Iceland. When it arrived uneventfully in London the following day, it became the first civilian land-plane to have crossed the Atlantic in scheduled airline service.

The crossing was notable for another reason. It was flown not by Pan American, which had held a near-monopoly among U.S. carriers on international service before World War II, but by American Overseas Airlines, a new-comer to the ranks of international airlines. The airplane AOA used for the flight had been a military C-54 cargo plane until a few weeks before, when it was hastily converted into a DC-4 for its historic civilian debut. It was called *Flagship New England* and carried a bright orange-red trim, telltale signs that AOA was majority owned by American Airlines.

World War II's effect on commercial aviation was exponential. Foremost it left a legacy of major technical advances that would have taken several peacetime decades to accomplish. Flying a large cargo or passenger plane from

New York to London across the forbidding North Atlantic or from Miami to Calcutta, India, via South America, Africa, and the Middle East had become almost as reliable as taking a transcontinental train. The war's vora-cious appetite for aircraft had also led to the perfection of mass production techniques that broke the onerously expensive cost structure of building airliners in small, prewar numbers. At the outbreak of World War II there were about 300 DC-3s in service worldwide. By the end of the war there were more than 11,000. In 1941, when America entered the war, the DC-4 was still a work in progress. By 1945 there were more than 1,600 of them flying. Though the general public was yet to realize it, the airplane as mass transportation had arrived.

The war also altered the balance between the airline industries of Europe and the United States. Europe's airlines were devastated by the war in spite of the scrappy fight many of them put up on both sides of the conflict to fly severely reduced schedules throughout the hostilities. The airlines would make their comeback relatively quickly in the postwar years, but Europe's airline manufacturing industry suffered a sadder fate. It had been on the verge of introducing advanced designs that promised to rival the best airliners America had to offer, but the war had turned these prospects to dust. There would be bright spots such as the Vickers Viscount turboprop, the Sud Avion Caravelle jet, and the supersonic Concorde, but civilian aircraft manufacturing on the scale of Airbus Industrie would be a long time coming.

America's airlines had a much better war. They formed the backbone of the U.S. armed forces' Air Transport Command, which blos-somed into a global enterprise of epic propor-tions. The domestic airlines provided essential war service in their own livery and also flew directly for the armed services. But they were also given a challenge that stretched their abilities to the limit and broke new ground. They were directed to join Pan American, which couldn't handle the skyrocketing demand alone, to establish large-scale air cargo and priority transport service to the various theaters of war worldwide.

At war's end Pan American had to contend with changing realities. Its beloved flying boats had been marginalized, and its jealously guarded near-monopoly among U.S. carriers on overseas routes had been cracked. It had to accept competition from other U.S. airlines rewarded by the American government with international routes for their wartime service. American and TWA were allowed into Europe. TWA was also permitted to serve the Middle East and India, and in 1950 it changed its name from Transcontinental and Western Air to Trans World Airlines. Braniff was let into South America, and Northwest was granted a northern route to the Far East. United Airlines gained rights to Hawaii. While not an international route, it was quite a coup against another Pan American monopoly. In coming years other airlines would follow United on the lucrative route to Hawaii.

The propliner boom was also boosted by an era of unprecedented economic prosperity in America that followed the war within a few years and sent demand soaring for business and leisure travel by air. And when the airliners went shopping for new equipment, Douglas, Lockheed, and Boeing were ready to indulge them.

The unpressurized DC-4 proved to be the first of Douglas' rubber-band airliners, so called because the basic fuselage was constantly stretched and mated to larger wings and more powerful engines to accommodate more passengers and increase performance. It was soon overshadowed by the pressurized Lockheed Constellation, a masterpiece of aerodynamics considered by many to be one of the most graceful airplanes ever built. Douglas responded with the pressurized DC-6 and the two firms were off on a tit for tat competition to outdo each other with new, improved models. This competition was to last a decade and end with the ultimate propliners, the DC-7C and the Lockheed Jetstream, the first airliners capable of consistently crossing either America or the Atlantic nonstop in both directions.

Boeing built only one postwar propliner, the eighty-six-seat B-377 Stratocruiser, developed from the pressurized, super-long-range

B-29 Superfortress bomber. With its fat fuselage the Stratocruiser was the most spacious of the postwar airliners and the best loved by the flying public; it captured a disproportionate amount of media attention with its famous downstairs bar. But the fuselage created a lot of drag, overcome only by extra power, which made the Stratocruiser uneconomical to operate compared to its sleeker if more cramped

British South American Airways linked the large expatriate British business community in South America with Britain in the immediate aftermath of World War II. The company initially flew Lancastrians, hastily converted four-engined Lancaster heavy bombers, and later the Avro York, a more comprehensive development of the Lancaster. A York had disappeared over the Andes in bad weather and attracted considerable recent interest when a team of mountaineers and researchers succeeded in finding its remains.

LUFTHANSA

As air travel became routine, the airlines provided an important link between parents working abroad and their children left at home in boarding schools or with relatives. Children traveling independently under the supervision of airline staff were in for a grand adventure. Many of them acquired a lifetime love of travel when they took their first unaccompanied flight on a school vacation to visit parents based far away.

airlines combined carried sixteen million. Back in 1932 they had carried only 474,000. The surge in air travel was so high by the early 1950s that the infrastructure had difficulty keeping up. For the first time the airlines were subjected to widespread passenger discontent with crowded terminals, packed airplanes, and insufferable delays before the industry managed to catch up and recover its dignity.

Tourists soon rivaled the importance of business travelers for the airliners. Mostly they were seeking the sun. The airlines brought mass tourism to Florida and turned it into a year-round destination. Southern California, the Southwest, and Hawaii also came within the means of large numbers of the modestly well-to-do, and cities like New York, Washington, D.C., and Chicago also got their share of visitors by air. Inevitably, the increased demand for affordable flying led to the introduction of coach class.

On international routes Pan American remained the preeminent U.S. carrier, flying a mixed fleet made by all three major manufacturers. As early as 1947 it introduced the first scheduled round-the-world flight. It established service to major cities in Europe, served West Africa, and continued on to Johannesburg, South Africa. It had a robust network linking the Middle East and the Far East, and fully realized its prewar transpacific ambitions, including service to Sydney, Australia.

Trans World Airlines competed aggressively with Pan American on the international routes. Privately owned by billionaire Howard Hughes, TWA billed itself as the airline to Hollywood's stars. It spared no expense to glamorize air travel and projected its prestige U.S. transcontinental service to many European destinations and beyond, to points east. The red and white livery of its Lockheed Constellations became as symbolic of American prosperity as Pan Am's blue globe. Pan American's attempts to be granted domestic U.S. rights were rebuffed by the government.

Curiously, not all American carriers shared the enthusiasm to go global. In spite of its auspicious start, American Airlines soon sold AOA to Pan American, preferring to concentrate on domestic business. United turned down the opportunity to serve the Pacific for the same reason.

At the end of World War II Europe's national airlines recovered rapidly, some with U.S. aid, and were supported by their own governments in the national interest. Placing

competitors. Only fifty-five were made, but it remained in service for years on such prestige runs as San Francisco–Hawaii, where the airlines could fill them with premium fares attracted by the plane's luxury.

In 1949 American Airlines became the world's first airline to carry more than three million passengers in one year and all U.S.

the flag before economics resulted in a spider web of bilateral routes that linked the globe's most exotic destinations, including thinly traveled segments that would not have been served on commercial grounds alone.

Imperial Airways returned in every respect except in name. It had been merged with prewar British carriers serving Europe into two sister companies: British Overseas Airways Corporation (BOAC) flew the long-haul routes, and British European Airways (BEA) served the continent. Air France, KLM, and Sabena were also quick to pick up their traditional route networks within Europe and overseas and establish new ones. A major development was the commencement of services to North America. By 1955 even Lufthansa was back and soon regained its prewar stature.

New reciprocal links were also forged by an increasing number of flag carriers to South America, Africa, Asia, and Australia on new routes made possible by the new propliners. New national airlines were formed and carriers infrequently seen in the past ventured further afield. Scandinavian Airlines System, a consortium national carrier representing Sweden, Denmark, and Norway, grew into a leading global line. SAS pioneered the polar route from Europe to California in DC-6Bs, shaving a third off the forty-hour time enroute the long way around.

Tourist class slashed ticket prices, making international air travel widely affordable for the first time. The rising demand for low-cost flights also saw the birth of the no-frills charter industry, eagerly embraced by a growing army of tourists in North America, Europe, and across the Atlantic. In 1957 for the first time more people crossed the Atlantic by air than by boat.

Mostly the world bought American equipment during the propliner era. For most long-haul needs Douglas, Lockheed, and Boeing were the only choice, and for short-haul flights there were all those surplus DC-3s and later the new Convair Metroliners. Britain tried to buck the trend with several home-grown airliners made in limited numbers, including the four-engined, fifty-passenger Handley Page Hermes, used primarily by BOAC, and shorter-range regional aircraft, such as the Vickers Viking. BOAC's slow, majestic Sandringham flying boats rumbled on between Britain and Australia until 1950 concurrent with modern Lockheed Constellation landplanes until enough Constellations were delivered to end the grand flying boat tradition in the interest of speed. The Soviet Union laid the foundations of its civil airline industry with the Li-2, a license-produced DC-3, and developed the rugged thirty-two-seat Ilyushin-14 twin-engined propliner for its vast socialist empire, and first tentative forays abroad.

The propliners reached their zenith with the Douglas DC-7C and the Starliner, last of the Lockheed Constellations. They crossed the Atlantic nonstop and linked Europe with California in twenty hours via the North Pole. Piston power had reached its limits. Propellers couldn't be made to rotate faster as their tips approached the speed of sound. No more rows of pistons could be added to boost power without increasing the risk of engine failure to unacceptable levels. But even before the Seven Seas and the Starliner made their debut there was another sound in the air, the shrill squeal of jet turbines powering the next generation of airliners, which would change air travel as profoundly as the propliners had in their time.

Experience gained from massive, global military air transport operations undertaken in World War II placed America's airlines on a whole new footing when peace came. New four-engined propliners carrying more than twice the load of the DC-3s twice as far at higher speeds were ready to flood the airways pioneered in the previous two decades, and even more capable airliners were in the works. Here a Pan American DC-4 drops in on a postwar Rio carnival, one of the best places to flee from Europe's devastation. The artist is von Arenburg.

Air France recovered quickly from the ravages of World War II, acquiring Lockheed's gorgeous Constellation and launching it on the Paris–New York route. The first transatlantic services made stops in Ireland, Iceland, and Gander, Newfoundland, and the typical crossing at this time was a twenty-five-hour affair, lightning fast compared to the boats, flying or floating.

This World War II American Airlines poster by Ivan Dimitri is one of the first examples of a photo poster. Here American Airlines is doing its part for the war effort around the clock, suggested by the night departure, speeding military officials and civilians alike on important missions in a time of crisis.

UNITED AIR LINES

NEW ENGLAND

Many pilots who learned their craft in the wartime DC-3s pictured on the previous page went on to fly the propliners that soon blanketed the United States and the world when peace came. United had the opportunity to acquire international routes after the war but preferred to remain a domestic airline. It vied for the top spot with American, which briefly flew to Europe immediately after the war but sold its routes to Pan American by 1950 in a move seen by many as a misstep. United's inviting New England scene is indicative of the increasing importance of tourism to the airlines.

Paris–New York was the most glamorous air route during the propliner era of the 1950s, enticing travelers to both destinations with discretionary delights only dreamed of elsewhere. When Transcontinental and Western Air was rewarded with international routes for its wartime services, it set out to give Pan American a run for its money and soon changed its name to Trans World Airlines. After using several DC-4s in its initial international fleet, TWA flew Lockheed Constellations exclusively on its long-range international routes until the jet era. Below, one of the first classes of French TWA stewardesses poses for the camera.

THE VIKING LINES

DANISH AIR LINES

DDL

DET DANSKE LUFTFARTSELSKAB

The stylish, long-range four-engined propliners grabbed all the headlines in the 1950s, but the era also saw the development of less glamorous, short-haul workhorses. Here the Danish airline DDL showcases its aptly named twin, the Vickers Viking, made in Britain and used throughout DDL's European network. DDL would shortly become one of the founding airlines of SAS, the Scandinavian Airlines System consortium owned jointly by Denmark, Sweden, and Norway, and still going strong.

By the 1950s flying was fun and the airliner a means of escape available on short notice, to whisk you away for a brief getaway or comfortably fly you all the way around the world in a couple of weeks. Acapulco was one of many resorts that benefited immensely from the expansion of the airlines and grew with them. The artist is Fred Ludenken.

Pan American was quick to promote tourism by air. This Caribbean poster by Jean Carlu entices visitors to traditional Pan Am territory that would soon be transformed by the airplane into one of the world's biggest mass-market tourist destinations. The airplane is an early-model Constellation, considered by many to be the most graceful of them all. It was flown by Pan Am on its inaugural round-the-world flight in 1947.

The long route down to South Africa was flown in cooperation by South African Airways and BOAC. Flying through the night the airlines' modern landplanes significantly reduced the transit time compared to the old Imperial Airways flying boats, although some passengers missed the flying boat's roominess in spite of the impeccable onboard service on their replacement.

A poster by Villemot promotes France for the home airline. Note the country's outline in the scene behind the Eiffel Tower filled with the best-known landmarks from the City of Light. Villemot had a contract with Air France in the 1940s and 1950s, but is best known for his later ad campaigns for such consumer goods as Orangina and Bally shoes. The Constellation in the poster is almost incidental. The focus is on the destination.

Here is an innovative perspective of New York City from Braniff International Airways. When landing at La Guardia passengers at the window seats could sometimes get the same perspective though not at such close range. The silhouette is that of a Douglas DC-6.

This view of a Japanese temple entrance is one in a series of destination posters painted by the renown aviation artist Frank Wootton for the British Overseas Airways Corporation, successor to Imperial Airways. The aircraft is a Handley Page Hermes, Britain's postwar entry into the propliner race designed to compete with the Douglas and Lockheed lines. The competition had a slight performance edge, and the Hermes wasn't developed beyond the initial design.

Air France's image-makers continued to rely on the air mail theme for decades in the form of various white carrier pigeons and pigeon parts in the airline's posters. Here the river Seine and an adjoining boulevard fuse into a speedy carrier pigeon. Another poster that occasionally appears on the poster circuit envelops the South American continent with a similarly shaped pigeon wing. The artist is Regis Manset.

Quantas Empire Airways was quick to adopt the swift Lockheed Constellation between Sydney and London, but BOAC, its partner on the route, also continued to use Sandringham flying boats until 1950. The arrangement made some sense as the regal, double-decked Sandringham continued to service the less active stops bypassed by the Constellations, until regional landplanes took over its role.

The airplane became a major mode of transportation in Eastern Europe and the Soviet Union in the 1950s. MASZOVLET was Hungary's airline founded in 1946 with Russian technical assistance and joint ownership. It started service with a fleet of Li-2s, license-produced Russian DC-3s. The leg to Peking across Mongolia looked impressive but was flown by Aeroflot. The Russians bowed out in 1954 and MASZOVLET became Malev Hungarian Airlines. Below in the rare photo from the late 1950s an Aeroflot Li-2 feeds passengers to a Tupolev TU-104, the jetliner that flew the world's first sustained scheduled jet service.

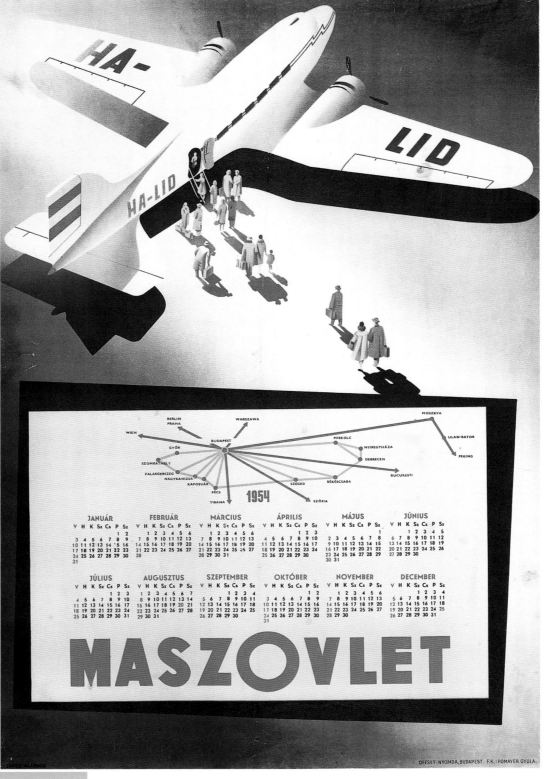

Southern California's playground beckons and the best way to get there is in a United DC-6 from this 1950s poster. In addition to its traditional agribusiness heritage and Hollywood's glitter, California had become one of the world's most important industrial regions and tourist destinations, where United faced stiff competition, especially from TWA and American Airlines.

Northwest Airlines grew rapidly from a regional carrier into a major international airline flying the northern route to the Pacific. Its big break came from the experience it gained flying wartime ferry and transport missions to Alaska, which was rewarded with national and international routes and prompted the company to change its marketing name to Northwest Orient. Besides its flagship Boeing Stratocruisers, derived from the B-29 Superfortress bomber, it also flew Douglas and Lockheed propliners on its international routes.

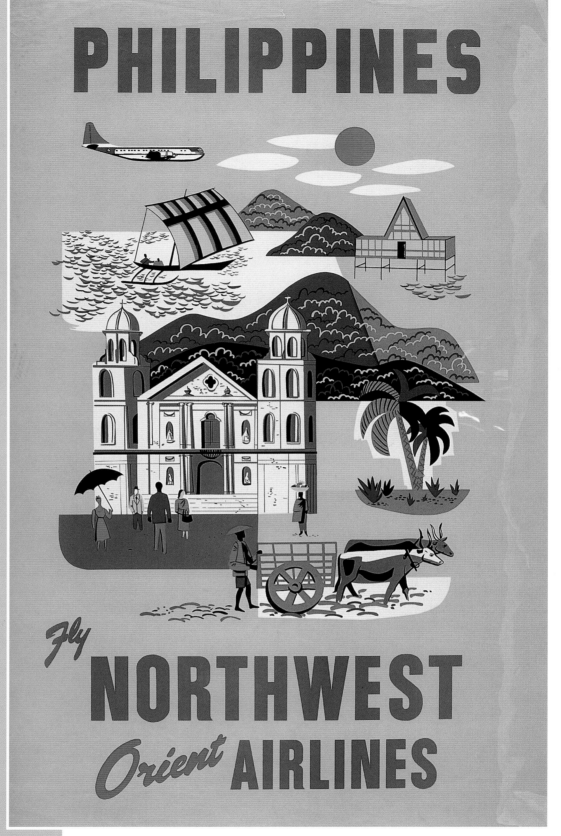

In the late 1940s and early 1950s Pan American realized its long-cherished goal of serving Europe's major destinations. This poster is one in a series that features the luxurious Boeing Stratocruiser introduced in 1949. It was popular with passengers who loved its cozy sleeping berths on the long nights across the Atlantic and the Pacific. But the Stratocruiser was technically cantankerous and less economical than its sleeker competitors and only fifty-five were built. Over a thousand served with the U.S. Air Force as air-to-air tanker aircraft.

Propliner Splendor 107

Although Holland lost its Indonesian colonies after World War II, KLM continued to grow and became a major global airline as the modern propliners came on stream. As for many other airlines, New York was one of its prime destinations, which it was the first non-U.S. airline to serve with the Constellation. This poster from the 1940s seems to play on the theme of leaving the old world's night for the new world's day.

Braniff, a fairly staid regional airline with no international ambitions prior to World War II, found itself thrust into South America on the express orders of President Truman in 1947, who was put off by patrician Pan Am's brazen attempts to keep other carriers off the international airways. The Texan regional hastily inserted "International" between "Braniff" and "Airways," printed some posters, and set out to find Rio. Within a few years its DC-6s and DC-7s were a familiar sight along the airways of South America.

North Africa continued to be an important market for Air France, driven both by government and commercial demand and by a steady growth in tourism. This cheerful Villemot poster from 1948 seems to be aimed at encouraging pleasure travel. The airplane is probably a Languedoc, a French regional airliner used on short- to medium-haul routes.

California was an important market for American Airlines, which was one of the three original airlines awarded a transcontinental route in the 1930s by the government. Los Angeles–New York was the Flagships' flagship service. In the photograph below Walt Disney is about to board a DC-6 for New York.

Pan American gained African experience flying for Air Transport Command in World War II. After the war it established service down to Johannesburg, South Africa, via the Azores and stops in West Africa. The leopard captures the popular imagination, but the business conducted in the modern buildings in the background was the primary reason for serving Johannesburg.

WASHINGTON

AMERICAN
AIRLINES

Washington, D.C., and its
incessant stream of traveling
politicians, bureaucrats,
lobbyists, and tourists has
always been a steady market
for America's airlines. The
Capitol, portrayed here by
E. McKnight Kauffer in 1950,
appears in practically every
airline poster featuring the
city. Airplanes leaving
Washington, D.C., tended
to be particularly packed
toward the end of the
week, like the DC-4 in the
accompanying photograph.

Hawaii had always been a playground for the rich, but from the 1950s the airplane made it accessible to a middle class ready to spend its increasing income on balmy beach vacations. The route was pioneered by Pan American's flying boats, but at the end of World War II government regulators opened it to United, which was quick to capitalize on the lucrative route.

The morning light flooding a Bavarian village is effectively captured by von Arenburg in this poster enticing Americans to Europe. Pan American also flew DC-6s and DC-7s to Europe and had the concession to serve West Berlin, isolated deep behind the Iron Curtain at the time.

These colorful toucans are the objective of the affluent tourists high above them on their way to South America in the SAS DC-6. The poster is one of a series by Otto Nielsen portraying the worldwide destinations of SAS. The airline pioneered the polar route from Europe to the U.S. West Coast with DC-6s, cutting a third off the thirty-plus-hour traditional roundabout route. The DC-4 on a rainy European ramp in the accompnying photograph is a powerful incitement to seek sunnier climates.

Ireland was a popular refueling stop for airliners before they could reach the European mainland nonstop, but as air travel became more affordable it also became a mass tourist destination. TWA's Celtic cross poster featured several types of Lockheed Constellations over the years. Here it shows a late-model Super Constellation. Dublin Airport was the first to open a duty-free shop.

Beirut is rarely thought of these days as a choice tourist destination, but in the 1950s it was a sophisticated yet exotic city where thousands of years of Mediterranean antiquity converged with modern Europe. The hours tended to drag on the long propliner flights between the United States and the Middle East, and in the Boeing Stratocruiser passengers vied with each other to spend at least some of their time in the famed downstairs bar, for which the airplane is best remembered by travelers.

GATEWAY TO THE MIDDLE EAST AND THE HOLY LAND

BEIRUT
LEBANON

by Clipper

PAN AMERICAN WORLD AIRWAYS
WORLD'S MOST EXPERIENCED AIRLINE

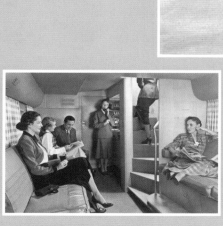

New York's skyscrapers lent themselves to this cubist interpretation by Weimer Pursell in 1956. American has a long history with New York, dating back to its transcontinental sleeper service out of Newark Airport in 1936, for which it convinced Douglas to design the DST that in day-service version became the DC-3. American also had its headquarters in Manhattan until 1979, when it relocated to Dallas–Fort Worth.

C^{IE} GÉNÉRALE DE TRANSPORTS AÉRIENS - AIR ALGÉRIE

QUADRIMOTEURS D.C.4

PARIS - LYON - MARSEILLE
POUR
ALGER - ORAN

As developing countries increasingly asserted their independence they established their own national carriers, often with technical assistance from the major airlines. Here an Air Algerie DC-4 passes a more leisurely mode of transportation mid-Mediterranean. The same aircraft is seen in the photograph at Paris Orly airport.

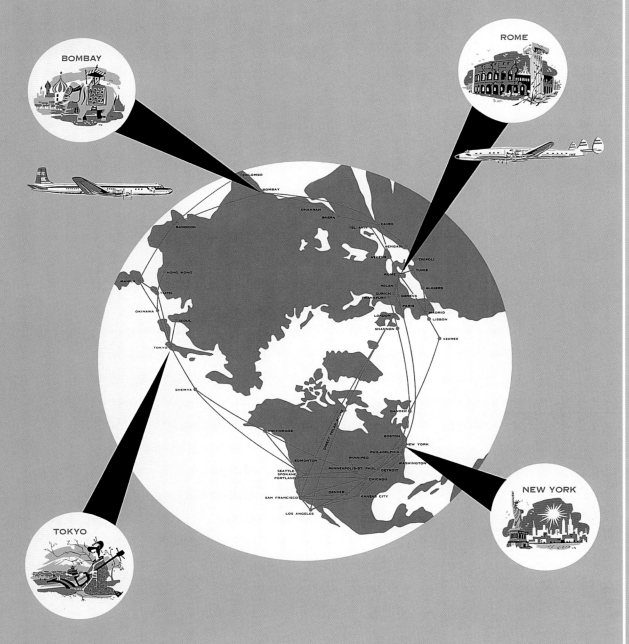

Northwest Orient and TWA collaborated in what today would be called a code-sharing agreement to provide a round-the-world flight, linking Northwest's Pacific network with TWA's international routes. The service competed with Pan American's famous Flight 1 (and Flight 2 in the opposite direction). Pan Am was first around the world in 1947 with its Constellations.

This TWA poster portrays all the reasons American tourists flocked to France in the 1950s: fashion, bistros, wine, museums, villages, cathedrals, mountains, the Med, and don't forget the Eiffel Tower; many of the same reasons we visit today. With tip tanks, TWA's Super Constellations were its first aircraft that could cross the Atlantic nonstop, but its fuel reserves were insufficient for scheduled nonstop service. That had to wait for the last model of TWA's Constellations, the Starliner.

Originating from privately owned Tata Airlines of the 1930s, Air India was formed after India gained independence from Britain in 1947. The airline quickly developed an extensive network covering Asia and Europe, and extended its London service across the Atlantic to New York. It flew Lockheed Constellations until the jet age, when it became one of the first operators of the Boeing 707 and later the Boeing 747.

The San Francisco street car has been featured in many airline posters over the years. United's roots in San Francisco reach back to when the city became its western base for its first transcontinental service in 1929. By the 1950s propliner cockpits had amassed a formidable array of bells and whistles to safely reach their destinations in most weather conditions. The DC-7 cockpit shown in the photograph below was more demanding on the flight crew than the much more automated cockpits of today's jetliners, which have enabled airliners to dispense with the services of the flight engineer.

American Airlines was one of the first airlines to grasp the commercial attraction of large-scale air freight services. American established a transcontinental freight division in 1944 and operated a scheduled network with a fleet of Douglas freighters, later replaced by Boeing jets. This is one of several posters for American by Weimer Pursell. Note the absence of windows on the freight DC-6 in the photograph.

In addition to its international routes, Air France has always had an extensive domestic network. This powerful poster by Eric, created in 1949, advertises the attractions of Corsica. The large, wild, mountainous Mediterranean island has always attracted the more adventurous visitors and is also know for a long-running separatist insurrection against mainland French control.

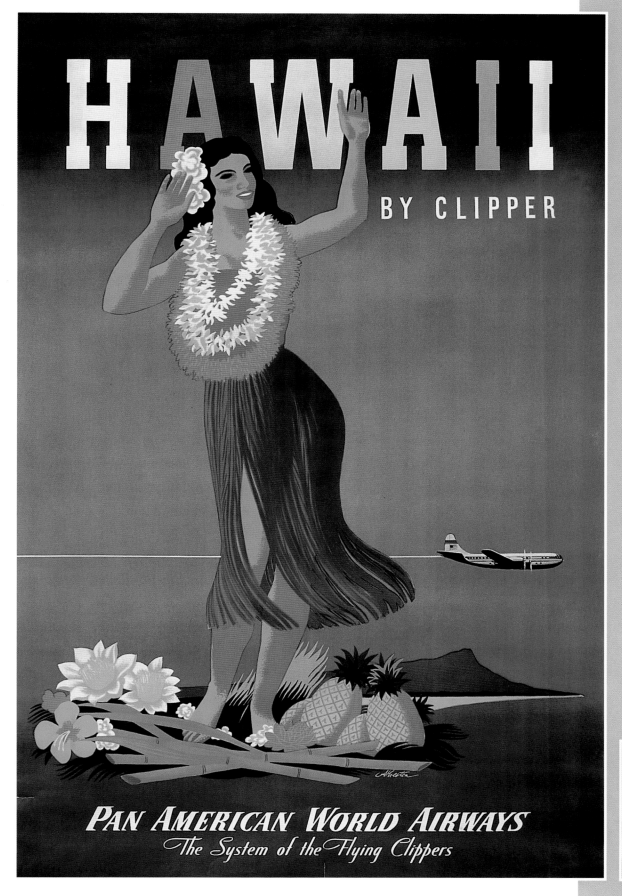

Here is one of Pan American's versions of the hula girl, timeless star of the Hawaiian airline posters. In the photograph Pan American and United Stratoliners are lined up in Honolulu shortly after arrival from the mainland. Stepping off a Stratoliner in the morning in Hawaii after sleeping through the night in a comfortable berth was a moment cherished by many passengers, although berths were becoming scarce by the 1950s as economic pressures mounted to increase passenger loads.

E. McKnight Kauffer created a series of posters for American Airlines in 1950. American was first across the Atlantic with a landplane after it won several European routes following World War II, but soon after this poster came out it relinquished its international presence to concentrate on the United States and its immediate neighbors. The DC-4 in the photograph below is performing a Jet Assisted Take Off (JATO) from a high-altitude airport in Mexico, assisted by a pair of small jet packs to more easily gain altitude. The technique was a short-term fix until higher performance engines were available.

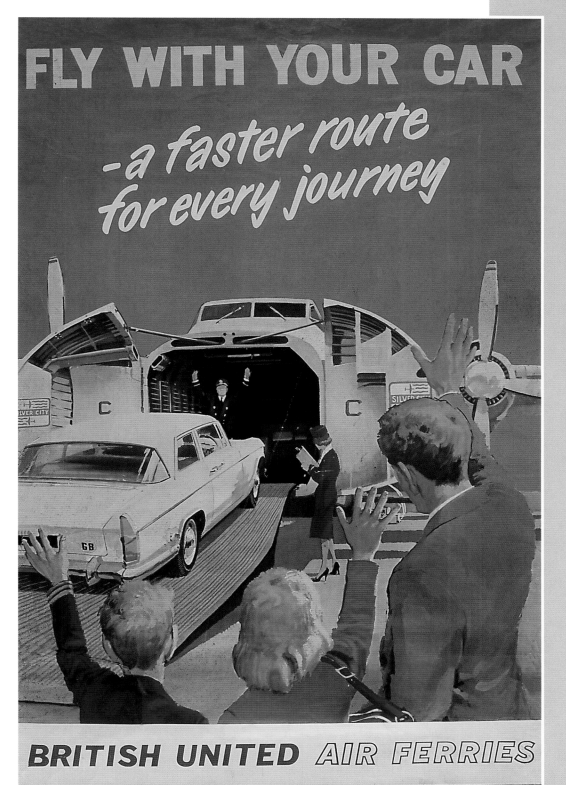

In the late 1950s and early 1960s Britons in a hurry to visit the continent with their cars could take the Silver City car ferry. They could drive onboard a Bristol Freighter and drive off into France about a half an hour later. Each aircraft had room for three cars and fifteen passengers. The service was put out of business by the cross-Channel Hovercraft, which could cross as fast and charge less per car. Silver City was bought by British United just after these posters were printed; hence the stripe with the new name. British United eventually merged with Caledonian to form British Caledonian. *Courtesy John Pothecary*

This Swissair poster commemorates the commencement of service to New York, launched with DC-4s after World War II. It is an outstanding example of International style developed by Swiss poster artists in the postwar years. The photographs of the airplane and Rockefeller Center are combined with crisp, modern typography to convey a powerful advertising message.

UNITED AIR LINES

Hawaii

United's poster of this Hawaiian dugout with Diamond Head in the background is a coveted collectors' item. An airplane is nowhere to be seen. It has come to be taken for granted. As the 1950s were coming to an end an increasing number of airline posters focused exclusively on the destination, relying only on their name to make the connection to air travel.

Two route maps show the extent of airline networks worldwide by the late 1950s. KLM's propliners served half the countries of the world on every continent except Antarctica, and Quantas made it all the way around the globe. Neither Holland nor Australia is particularly populous, yet their far-flung commercial and cultural interests and historic ties justified their national carriers' extensive services and the government subsidies required to sustain them.

Britain's Vickers Viscount turboprop was the harbinger of the great piston-engined propliners' demise. The shrill jet turbines that turned its propellers could be heard as early as 1953, and it went on to become the most successful modern British-built airliner. The many airlines that flew it included British European, Air France, Lufthansa, Alitalia, United, Continental, South African Airways, and others. The turboprop was a transition aircraft to the pure jet, but in short-haul commuter use, where it is most efficient, it began yielding to the pure jet only during the late 1990s.

CONTRAILS AROUND THE WORLD

Mrs. Clive Runnells of Lake Forest, Illinois, had a lunch date at the Ritz in Paris, France, on October 27, 1958, but the evening before she was still in New York. That was cutting it a bit close for those days, but Mrs. Runnells wasn't unduly concerned. She had a ticket on Pan American's evening flight to Paris, the first scheduled jet flight by an American airline. At 7:20 that night, after a reception at Idlewild Airport hosted by Juan Trippe, Pan American's founder and CEO, Mrs. Runnells and 110 fellow travelers boarded the company's first Boeing 707 jetliner, the *Clipper America*, and blasted off for the City of Light.

They made it in eight hours and fifteen minutes, half the time it took the fastest propliners to cross, and that even included a refueling stop (which was needed by the first batch of 707s). Mrs. Runnells had plenty of time to stroll through the boutiques around the Place Vendome before making her lunch appointment. Then, mission accomplished, she boarded Pan American's return flight and flew back to New York to complete her small part in ushering in the jet age.

The jetliner era had actually begun six years earlier, but it was an abortive start. The British de Havilland Comet was the world's first passenger jet, and in 1952 it took off in BOAC colors on its maiden scheduled flight from London to Johannesburg, South Africa. After three years of flight tests the shrill, winged bullet of an airplane that had enthralled the public and electrified the headlines looked set to reap the benefits of Britain's postwar lead in jet technology. The trip was a spectacular success. The Comet arrived on schedule in only twenty-three hours via stops in Rome, Beirut, Karthoum, Entebbe, and

Livingstone. It had shaved seventeen hours off the forty-hour journey by propliner.

For the next eighteen months BOAC's Comets broke speed records throughout the company's Asian and African routes, but then disaster struck. A series of catastrophic accidents at high altitude grounded the Comets and it took six years to discover and re-engineer the structural weakness in the fuselage that had caused them to explode.

The setback left just enough room for others to seize the initiative. Aeroflot, the Soviet Union's national carrier, established the world's first sustained jet service in 1956 with Tupolev TU-104s. And Pan American prodded late-comers Boeing and Douglas to launch the Boeing 707 and the Douglas DC-8, the two jetliners that would turn the jet age into big business.

With room for as many as 120 passengers each, both American jets were bigger than the 36-seat Comet I. They had longer range, were more economical to operate, and except for the first few 707s, they could cross the Atlantic non-stop. So while the Comet series made a modest comeback after its redesign, the long-haul world largely belonged to the Boeing 707 and the Douglas DC-8 for the next two decades.

The airlines rushed to join the jet age. By 1959 Boeing and Douglas shared orders for 350 jetliners and had already delivered enough of them by 1960 to enable all of America's major carriers to make their jet debut. TWA's red-and-white 707s were becoming as familiar in foreign skies as Pan American's blue-and-white Jet Clippers, and the Boeing and Douglas jets were being sighted with increasing frequency in diverse foreign plumage. Air France, Lufthansa, Air India, Pakistan International Airlines, Quantas, BOAC, Sabena, Avianca, Varig, and the White House joined the 707 camp. KLM, Alitalia, SAS, Japan Air Lines, Swissair, Air Canada, and Iberia were among those who opted for the Douglas DC-8.

The jets' arrival stirred the popular imagination. Passengers flocked by the millions to fly them and spectators rushed to airports to watch them come and go with an enthusiasm not seen since the early days of the DC-3. The media quickly dubbed affluent frequent flyers the "jet set." The jet set was soon suffering fashionably from jet lag. Mrs. Runnells' transatlantic lunch stunt inspired copycats. One New York socialite jetted to Paris to get her hair done for a ball. For the first time couples flew to Europe for the weekend. And they all raved about the smooth, quiet ride high above the propliner traffic where air sickness was a rarity.

But in spite of the jet set's grab for the headlines, the arrival of the jets was a great social leveler that opened the floodgates to mass air travel. Rapid increases in engine performance and fuel efficiency came from the introduction of the fan-jet engine, a landmark step beyond the basic fuel guzzlers. It increased the jetliners' range and enabled them to carry as many as 170 passengers per flight, twice the capacity of the top propliners, at twice the speed. Their better-than-expected mechanical reliability slashed maintenance needs compared to the propliners. It all added up to soaring productivity and capacity on the world's airways, and greater affordability. Everyone could keep up with the jet set on economy class.

And it struck a chord with the traveling public. Global air travel doubled in the two years following the maiden flight of *Clipper America*. By 1962 Boeing's 707s alone had carried more than thirty million passengers and thirty airlines offered transatlantic jet service. Icelandic, the first transatlantic budget airline, offered cut-rate jet fares between New York and tiny, centrally-located Luxembourg (which had no national carrier) via a stop in Iceland. Promotional summer fares siphoned vacationers away from traditional local and regional destinations to distant continents. One travel day each way left twelve days to explore Europe for Americans on a two-week vacation. Students with time on their hands could afford to spend a summer circling the globe on a youth fare.

While the DC-8 and the Boeing 707 had the lion's share of the long-haul market, other types also made their appearance and attracted a lot of attention. They included the super-fast Convair Coronado, which fell short of range

and fuel-efficiency expectations, and the elegant Vickers VC-10 with four aft-mounted engines.

The early jets made the most sense on long-haul routes where they could save the most time over the propliners. But some European manufacturers were motivated early in the jet game by Europe's shorter distances to develop medium-range jets. First came an interim hybrid solution in the early 1950s, the forty-four-seat Vickers Viscount turboprop. Its four jet engines turned four propellers,

TWA flew to India for decades starting in the 1940s. In the early 1970s India was a stop on TWA's round-the-world route, shortly after the airline was authorized by the U.S. Civil Aviation Board to cross the Pacific. However, it soon found the Pacific sector uneconomical and gave up these routes but continued to fly to India via Europe. David Klein's bejeweled elephant evokes the opulence of the maharajas' palaces, a strong draw on the tourist circuit.

South America with Flying Colors
Braniff International

giving them greater speed and efficiency over the piston-engined propliners on flights up to their 700-mile range. The Viscount became Britain's most successful airliner, exported widely, and deserves more credit than it generally gets. While it was superceded by medium-haul jets, smaller turboprops, including the F-27 made by a resurrected Fokker, remained viable in commuter service.

The first successful medium-range jet was the fifty-passenger French Sud Avion Caravelle, which entered service in 1959. Considered by many to be the most elegant airliner of its time with graceful curves left uncluttered by its two rear-mounted engines, it could turn a profit on flights as short as 200 miles. U.S. airlines were not known at the time for buying foreign aircraft, but several bought the Viscount and United bought twenty Caravelles.

Boeing did bring out a slightly shorter-range version of the 707, the 720, but took its time to intensively focus on the medium- and short-haul market along with its chief rival Douglas. But when they made this market a priority, they once again walked off with most of it for the next twenty years.

Boeing's 727, the first American trimotor since the Ford Trimotor of the 1920s, became the world's most-produced airliner during its lifetime, with more than 3,500 built. Its twin-engined contemporary, the Boeing 737, eventually overtook it and is still going strong in its latest variant. Douglas' entry, the DC-9, also became a global workhorse, ironically ending up as the Boeing 717 in its last variation when Boeing bought McDonnell Douglas in 1997.

The last two acts of commercial aviation to capture the popular imagination with any intensity resembling the age of Lindbergh were the introduction of the supersonic Concorde and the Boeing 747 jumbo jet. The Concorde revived for a time the glamour of air travel to a level unseen since the flying boats, but was a commercial failure. The behemoth Boeing 747 carried twice as many passengers as the 707, and matured into a runaway commercial success after the nasty scare of the 1973 oil crisis. But as its novelty wore off, any glamour that may have been left from the early days of going by air eroded as well. The journey ceased to be the reward. Passengers hopped on an airliner as casually as they boarded a bus. They could hardly wait for the flight to be over so that the adventure could begin. And increasingly, the more nostalgic among them began to collect the airline posters of the past.

Pan American was the first U.S. airline to fly jets when in 1958 it launched Boeing 707 service to Paris, France. Its 707s also signaled a new phase of growth in tourism to the Caribbean. Compared to the most advanced propliner, a 707 added as many as forty extra seats and reached its destination twice as fast, enabling the airline to rapidly increase capacity.

A powerful image by Nathan entices the traveler to Japan on Air France without any mention of the Boeing 707s the airline used to fly there as soon as they became available. In 1970 Air France and Japan Air Lines negotiated rights to fly to Tokyo over the Soviet Union, which was off limits to other western airlines and shortened the journey by several hours compared to the southern route via the Middle East, India, and Southeast Asia.

A Mexicana poster from 1960 announces the airline's entry into the jet club. The tiny jet high above the Yucatan's Mayan temples is a de Havilland Comet IV, one of five owned by the airline, inaugurated on Golden Aztec service between Mexico City and Los Angeles. The British Comet was the world's first jetliner but in most markets it lost out to the larger, more economical Boeing 707. Pan American, the world's first 707 operator, owned part of Mexicana until 1968. This poster is one in a series featuring the Comet IV (also shown in the photograph) over Mexico's ancient heritage sites.

Trans Australian Airways, the antipodean local carrier, was an enthusiastic early operator of turboprops, flying the Vickers Viscount, Lockheed Electra, and Fokker Friendship. All three provided jet reliability and faster speed across Australia's vast empty distances. The Viscount and Electra were soon made obsolete by such jets as the Douglas DC-9 and Boeing 727, but the smaller twin-engined Fokker commuter remained in production into the 1980s.

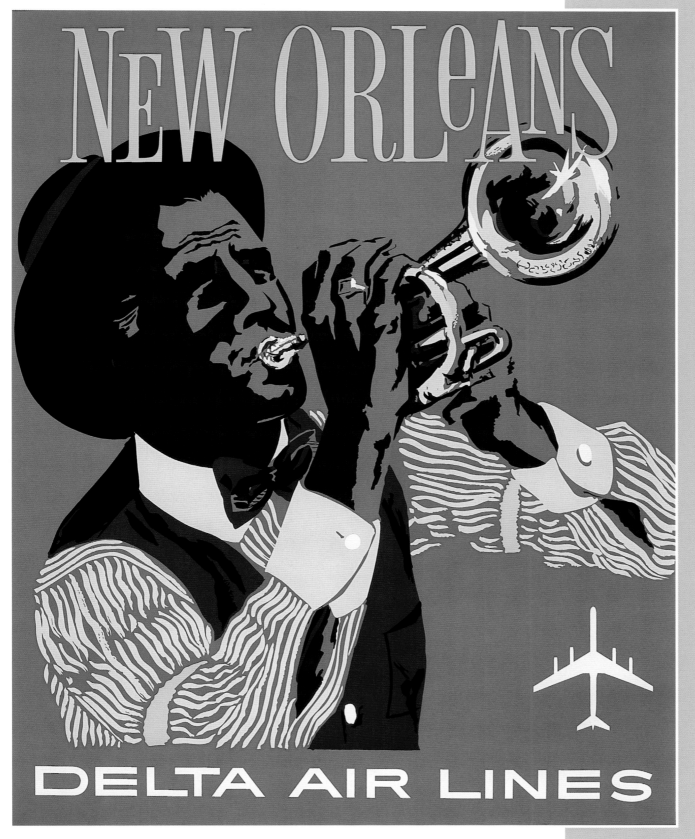

NEW ORLEANS

DELTA AIR LINES

Delta Airlines became the first airline to fly the Douglas DC-8 when it got a chance to pick up an order given up by its archrival, Eastern Airlines. Eastern unwisely decided to stick with its Lockheed Electra turboprops until a higher performance version of the DC-8 was available. Delta snapped up the order and passengers abandoned Eastern's Electras in droves to fly the DC-8. A favorite destination was New Orleans, drawing a steady stream of tourists, conventioneers, and business travelers.

The fireworks blaze around the Eiffel Tower as TWA introduces jet service with Boeing 707s in 1959. Actually, make that one Boeing 707, in domestic service. TWA was late in signing up for jets as its eccentric billionaire owner, Howard Hughes, got distracted with the Lockheed Starliner (called Jetstream by TWA), the Constellation's last incarnation. For the first few months the lonely 707 shuttled daily across the United States with such reliability that it maintained the illusion of being a small fleet. International service soon followed. The artist is David Klein, who painted a large series of posters for TWA at the beginning of the jet age. They are becoming collectors' items and steadily rising in price.

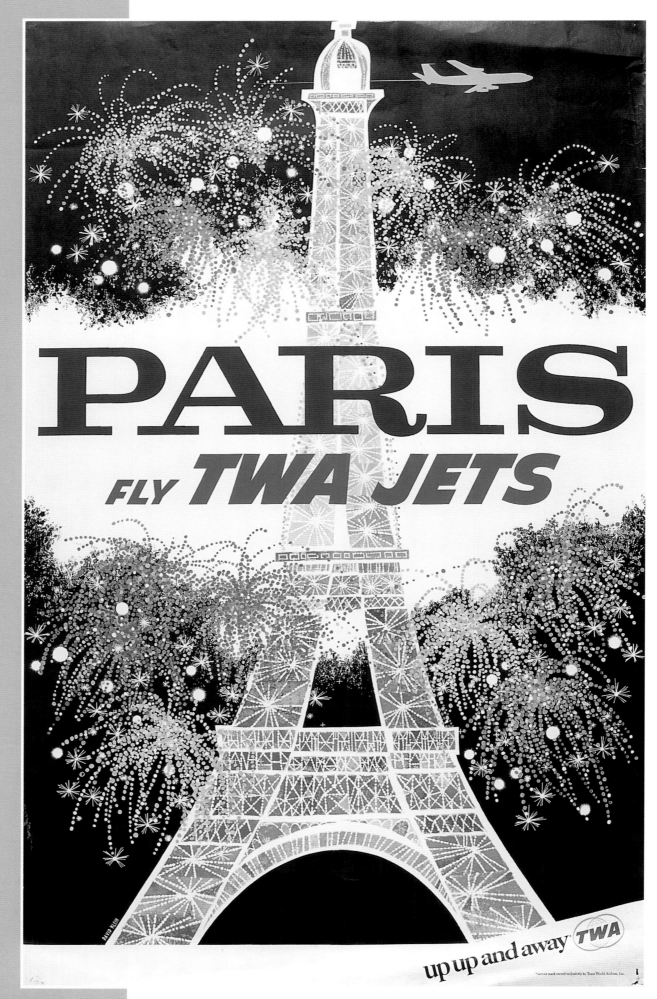

This 1960s Braniff poster nicely catches the essence of the Washington scene at the time. Note the shortage of women and a lack of minorities in the poster. With Lyndon Johnson in the White House and other powerful Texas politicians in Congress the mid-1960s was a busy time for Braniff between its home state and the capital. Braniff started jet service with Boeing 707s like the one pictured below, and in 1967 it inherited a Douglas DC-8 fleet when it bought PANAGRA from its feuding owners, Pan American and W. R. Grace Company.

Contrails around the World   143

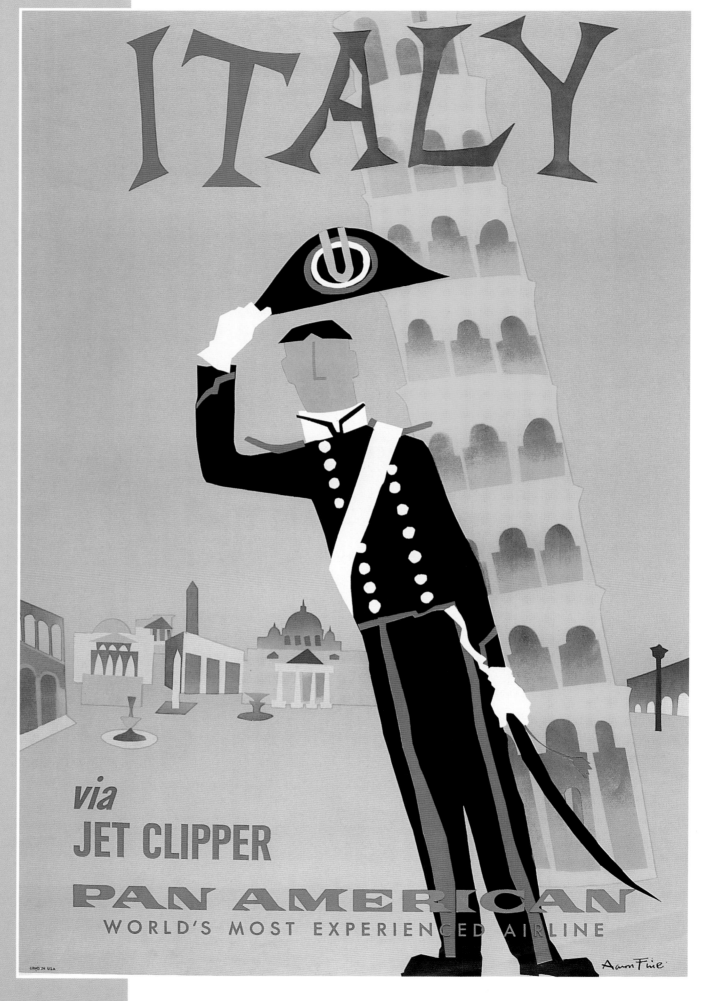

A whimsical Aaron Fine poster from the early 1960s features one of Italy's most recognizable monuments, the leaning tower of Pisa. Pan American didn't serve Pisa, but Rome was an easy gateway to all of Italy and the starting point of most visitors flying in from the United States to tour the country.

ZUR WELTAUSSTELLUNG
IN NEW YORK
MIT
TWA
JETS

Another David Klein poster advertises the 1964 New York World's Fair and TWA's jet service to the city. This version is aimed at travelers from Germany. Once the artwork was done, the image was often used with different messages for different purposes. Some images were re-issued year after year with updated information. The stewardess in the photograph below marches off enthusiastically into the jet age. Soon she would be known as a flight attendant.

Contrails around the World   145

Colombia's airline, Avianca, was quick to establish Boeing 707 service to the United States and Europe, and had an extensive network across its large, mountainous home ground, where surface transportation was slow and undeveloped. Avianca's roots go back to the 1920s and its German founders, who were forced out during World War II by Pan American. It is one of Latin America's most experienced airlines.

The boulevards of Paris radiate toward every corner of Europe from the Arc de Triomphe, and Air France's medium-range Caravelles were ready to whisk the visitor in any direction desired. Pictured here is the prototype Caravelle in formation with the first one delivered to Air France. Introduced in 1959, the Sud Avion Caravelle was one of the most graceful jets ever built, and a great pre-Airbus success for the French aviation industry. Even United Airlines flew a fleet of twenty Caravelles in the early 1960s.

Contrails around the World   147

Times Square would be unmistakable in this abstract poster, even without the script identifying New York, but for doubters confirmation comes in the form of the spotlight, the famous "ball" that drops every New Year's Eve at the stroke of midnight to usher in the new year. The poster, signed "David," is by David Klein.

This image, created in 1947 by Baudouin, shows the longevity and versatility of a well-done poster. Note the silhouette of the airplane. It is a Boeing 707 jet (also in the photograph) dating the poster to the early 1960s. The original poster had the outline of Air France's first Lockheed Constellation propliner. A clever silhouette change prolonged the life of one of Air France's most effective posters. The earlier edition is more highly valued by collectors.

Contrails around the World   149

American Airlines
Washington

The image has become somewhat abstract by the jet age, but the Capitol and the Washington Monument are clearly recognizable in this poster by Lawrence Gaynor. It is one of a series commissioned by American Airlines to feature its flagship destinations. American was one of the first airlines to commission series of posters from well-known artists to promote its flagship destinations.

CHICAGO
UNITED AIR LINES

Chicago is United Airlines' headquarters and long-time primary hub. In 1959, when United entered the jet age with Douglas DC-8s simultaneously with Delta, it set non-stop speed records in both directions between the Windy City and Hawaii to demonstrate the jet's capabilities.

Contrails around the World 151

Brazil's Varig Airlines is one of several airlines to serve South America's vast distances from the earliest days of air transportation. It flew Boeing 707s on its long-haul routes in the 1960s. Brazil is almost twice the size of Europe and its progress would have been severely restricted without heavy reliance on air travel. Varig's internal routes have always been as important to Brazil as its prestige runs to North America and Europe.

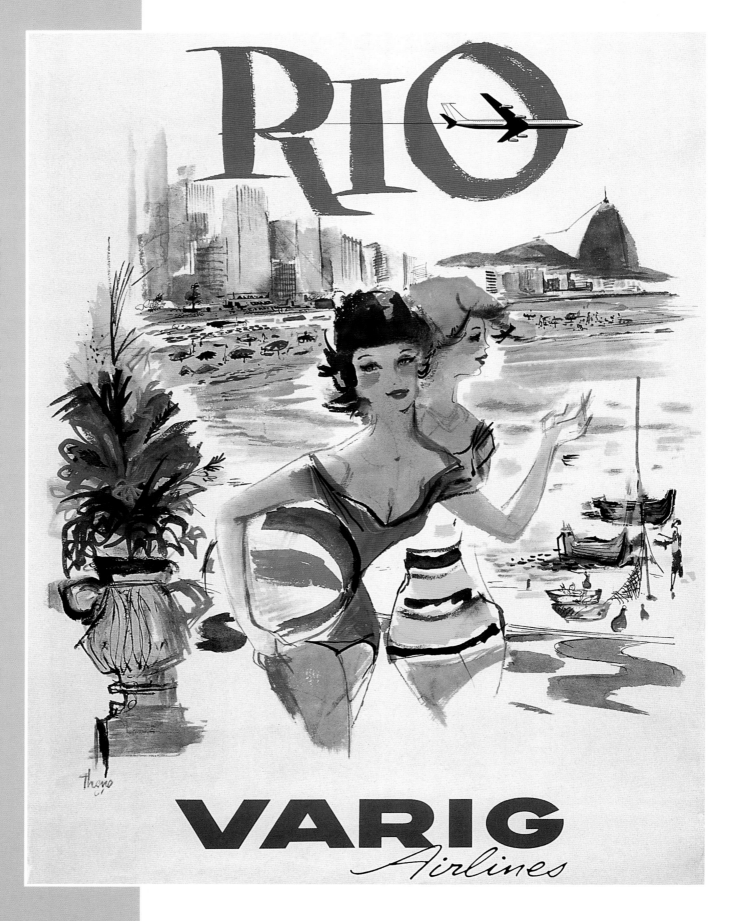

Africa

SABENA

belgian world airlines

Sabena built on its African heritage to develop an extensive network beyond Europe. In the 1960s African wildlife safaris were beginning to attract an increasing number of middle-class tourists as affluence rose not only in America but also in Europe and air travel became more affordable. Sabena's first-class travelers could still enjoy sumptuous meals in railroad-dining-car-style seating on their way to seek roaring lions, reminiscent of an earlier time.

Spain was one of TWA's most popular destinations. Glorified by the works of Ernest Hemingway and others, the bull fight was a prime tourist attraction, in spite of increasingly widespread concerns about animal welfare among Americans. David Klein's portrait captures the tension in the arena as the matador parades to face death in the afternoon.

mexicana ⋀

Bull fighting was also a regular feature on Mexican airline posters, painted by artists who specialized in the advertising posters that announced the events. Here a Mexicana Boeing 727 flies high over a bull fight portrayed in more conventional style than the image created by David Klein for TWA on the previous page. In the accompanying photograph a Mexicana 727, parked in front of Los Angeles airport's landmark restaurant, prepares for departure.

A British United
Airlines Vickers VC-10
flies over Mount
Kilimanjaro, Africa's
tallest mountain. BUA
was a scrappy private
airliner that did battle
with Britain's two state-
owned airlines: British
Overseas Airways
Corporation and
British European
Airways. It flew
throughout Europe
with a fleet of BAC
111s and to South
America and Africa
with VC-10s. BUA
later merged with
Caledonian to form
British Caledonian,
which grew into a
major international
airline before being
merged into today's
privatized British
Airways. *Courtesy
John Pothecary*

TWA's Boeing 707s could reach Switzerland nonstop, unlike the Constellations, and were twice as fast. For experienced passengers used to traveling by Constellation, switching to the 707 was an experience similar to the elation passengers felt in a later time when they took their first trip on Concorde after flying on subsonic jets for years.

In the 1960s Air India ran an ad campaign to promote maharaja service onboard the airline's Boeing 707s. It centered around a cuddly potentate and his mischievous adventures in the world's capitals served by Air India, implying that if the airline kept him happy and got him safely to his many destinations, passengers could expect the same regal treatment.

New Zealand's National Airways Corporation arranged one of the more unusual services for adventurous passengers. On an excursion to New Zealand's Southern Alps, long before the invention of packaged adventure travel and heli-skiing, they landed ski planes on a glacier near the summit of 12,350-foot Mount Cook, the country's highest peak. It was a chance to get an up-close taste of the mountains without having to climb for days, ideal for travelers in a hurry or the less athletic.

American travelers started visiting Egypt by the plane load on package tours during the 1960s. Minutes after alighting from their tour bus at the pyramids most found themselves hoisted on a camel's back by eager touts oblivious to shouts of "How much?" until the ride's end. David Klein's portrait of this dromedary was sure to strike a chord with any traveler who had the obligatory close encounter with a camel. In spite of jet speeds, the flight attendants pictured below had to pour a lot of champagne in first class before they reached Cairo.

SEE TEL-AVIV

AND FLY THERE WITH EL AL ISRAEL AIRLINES

By the 1960s Israel was sufficiently organized for tourism to attract leisure travelers. Tel Aviv's beaches were an ideal place to unwind from a rich diet of culture, history, archeology, and religious reflection offered by a land holy to three major religions. In peaceful times the region's rewards for the perceptive traveler are priceless. El Al, Israel's state airline, flew Constellations and turboprop Bristol Britannias to Europe and the United States before upgrading to the Boeing 707 when it became available.

Guy Georget's image of Greece is one of a series of Air France destination posters he created in 1963. Others include California, Mexico, the Near East, Spain, India, and Italy, all represented in bright, pop art colors in keeping with the times. The image of an airplane is absent in all of them.

GREECE

AIR FRANCE

Guy Georget

Portugal

In the sixteenth century Portuguese explorers sailed caravels similar to the fishing caravels in this poster to faraway continents little known to Europeans. In the 1960s another type of Caravelle was a regional workhorse of TAP, the Portuguese national airline.

 **TAP** Portuguese Airways

Russia was still the Soviet Union when TWA, along with Pan American, was granted route rights to Moscow in the 1970s and Aeroflot was allowed into the United States. Reciprocal air service was one of the first signs of thaw in the long, dreary Cold War. During its long association with Europe, TWA had a Europe-based fleet of Boeing 727s that connected with flights from the United States at European hubs. The image of the famed onion domes in Red Square is a good example of how photographs can be as forceful an element of posters as artwork.

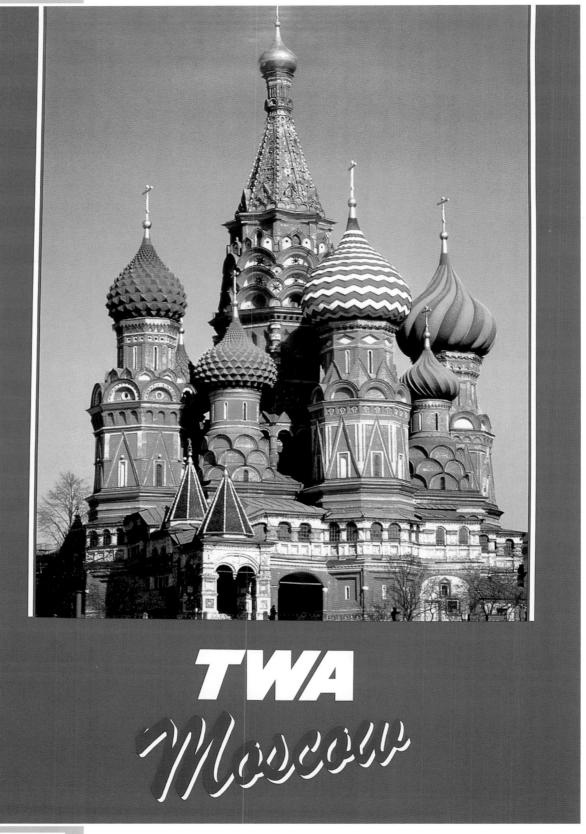

TWA
Moscow

A Boeing 707 soars high above San Francisco's Golden Gate Bridge, symbolic of the many airliners that have posed over this landmark since it was built. In addition to being an important West Coast transcontinental base, San Francisco was also a point of departure for TWA flights to Hawaii and its short-lived transpacific services.

Icelandic Air, known for a time as Islandic, pioneered bargain fares in the face of tightly regulated international ticket prices based on a series of bilateral agreements between country pairs. Icelandic flew between the United States and Luxembourg via a stop in Iceland and deeply undercut prices between the United States and other European destinations. This poster could be a bit misleading. At first glance it could imply that Icelandic is the Viking ship, rather than the only bargain alternative to the ship. In the 1960s and 1970s Icelandic's fleet included Douglas DC-8s and Boeing 727s.

IT'S NOT EASY TO BEAT ICELANDIC AIRLINES' PRICE TO EUROPE.

Icelandic
LOWEST JET FARES TO EUROPE OF ANY SCHEDULED AIRLINE.

PHOENIX

Western Airlines

This Western Airlines poster is a work of psychedelic art characteristic of the late 1960s. The style was widely used on record covers, music posters, and in other media. Western Airlines had an extensive network throughout the western United States with strong connections to the Midwest. Western kept some of its Boeing 720s long after most other airlines moved beyond them, preferring the slight additional operating expense in comparison to newer aircraft instead of a big capital expenditure on replacement aircraft. In 1987 Western merged with Delta.

Contrails around the World   167

A rare poster advertises Kuwait Airways' service to Sudan. Following traditional trading relationships and a common cultural heritage, airlines of Middle Eastern countries flew to a wide range of destinations along an east-west axis ranging from Africa to the Far East. In Africa they provided links eastward, complementing African connections northward to Europe.

As Las Vegas turned into America's racy gambling and entertainment capital its increasingly bright lights attracted as many airlines as could manage to get route allocations from the government to fly there prior to deregulation. Las Vegas was a lucrative destination for TWA. The airline's DC-9s were a familiar sight at McCarran Airport, within sight of the Vegas strip.

Tämä on Finnairin Kymppi.

DC-10 koneen suunnittelussa on kiinnitetty erityistä huomiota matkustajien mukavuuteen. Kymppiin mahtuisi 354 matkustajaa, mutta mukavuuden vuoksi siihen otetaan korkeintaan 294. Kympin moottorit on valmistanut General Electric ja niiden melutaso on varsin alhainen. Kympit lentävät reittiliikenteessä Helsingin ja New Yorkin välillä sekä pitkillä tilauslennoilla.

Matkustajamäärä	275/294
Pituus	55,47 m
Kärkiväli	49,17 m
Korkeus	17,70 m
Moottorit General Electric, lähtövoima	3×23130 kp
Kantama täydellä matkustaja-kuormalla	9800 km
Suurin matkalentonopeus	925 km/h
Matkatavara- ja rahti-kapasiteetti	41750 kg

This Finnair poster is a rare example of a modern airline poster that features an airliner. When Finnair got its first DC-10s, the behemoth widebodies were enough of a novelty to make a brief, introductory appearance in airline posters otherwise dominated by destinations. Finnair inaugurated its DC-10s on service to North America and also flew them to the Far East.

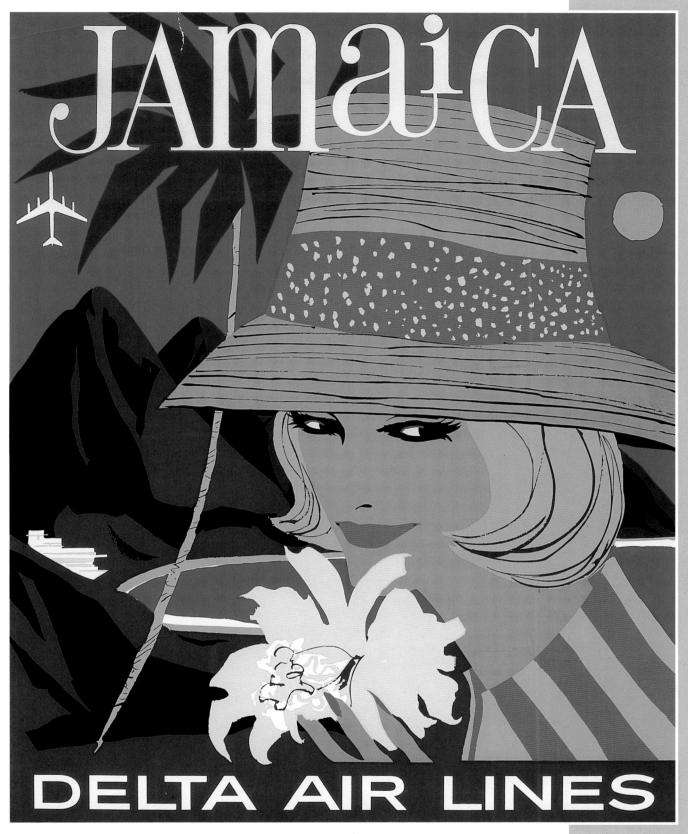

As America experiences a retro revival and the styles of the 1960s enjoy a comeback, Delta Airlines could get more mileage from this poster. All it would need to do is swap the silhouette of the DC-8 for an Airbus flown to the island by its codesharing partner Air Jamaica, and update the script. Delta's 727s were also seen in Jamaica from time to time.

In 1996 TWA celebrated a half a century of experience crossing the Atlantic. The contrast is stark between the Boeing 747 and the Lockheed Constellation that made the first crossing in 1946. It is also remarkable that by 1996 TWA had been flying the 747 for more than twenty years.

IF FIFTY YEARS OF EXPERIENCE ACROSS THE ATLANTIC HAS TAUGHT US ANYTHING, IT'S THAT YOU CAN'T REST ON FIFTY YEARS OF EXPERIENCE.

London Paris Lisbon  Madrid Barcelona Rome

Riyadh Tel Aviv Athens Milan Cairo Frankfurt

Portland

Continental
THE PROUD BIRD WITH THE GOLDEN TAIL

Portland, Oregon, was an important destination for Continental dating back to its first phase of national route expansion. The style of the artwork in this poster recalls those earlier days. The "Proud Bird with the Golden Tail" slogan refers to an ad line coined by Robert Six, the airline's flamboyant founder. He wanted to paint the entire fleet a metallic gold, but settled for golden tails when told that his idea was impractical.

Contrails around the World   173

Pan American celebrated its 50th birthday in 1977 with this poster that represents its significant achievements. The Fokker F-VII, the Boeing 747, and the airplanes in between speak for themselves. The following year Pan American was forced to enter the era of deregulation in a condition too flawed to survive by the new rules, but managed to struggle on for thirteen more years before lowering the final curtain on the greatest American airshow.

FOKKER F-7.
Pan Am's first plane. Made the first scheduled international flight by an American airline on October 28, 1927, between Key West, Florida and Havana, Cuba.

SIKORSKY S-38.
Versatile amphibian. Pioneered many routes for Pan Am® throughout Latin America.

SIKORSKY S-42.
America's first true transoceanic transport. Used mainly on Latin American routes, it also surveyed routes across Pacific and over Atlantic.

MARTIN M-130.
Inaugurated first scheduled flight across the Pacific. In November, 1935, flew from San Francisco to Manila in just under 60 hours flying time.

BOEING B-314.
Largest—and last—of Pan Am's flying boats. Opened the first regular transatlantic service in 1939. A vital carrier of men and supplies during World War II.

DOUGLAS DC-4.
Marked the transition to landplanes for transoceanic flights. Flew between United States and Europe, Asia, Latin America and Africa.

LOCKHEED CONSTELLATION.
Completed the first commercial round-the-world flight in 1947. The "Connie" was the first transatlantic aircraft with a pressurized cabin.

BOEING STRATOCRUISER.
Luxurious double-decker. Mainstay of Pan Am's transocean fleet from 1949 to 1958. Shown here on a special flight to Antarctica.

BOEING 707.
On October 26, 1958, a Pan Am Jet Clipper® flew from New York to Paris on the first scheduled jet flight by a U.S. airline. Soon afterwards Pan Am Jet Clippers were flying worldwide, revolutionizing air travel.

BOEING 747.
Introduced to the world by Pan Am in 1970. The largest, most comfortable, most reliable aircraft ever built. Carries over 370 passengers.

BOEING 747SP.
Newest Pan Am first. A shorter, faster, higher-flying version of the 747. Has the longest range of any commercial aircraft— up to 7500 miles nonstop.

50 years of experience
PAN AM.

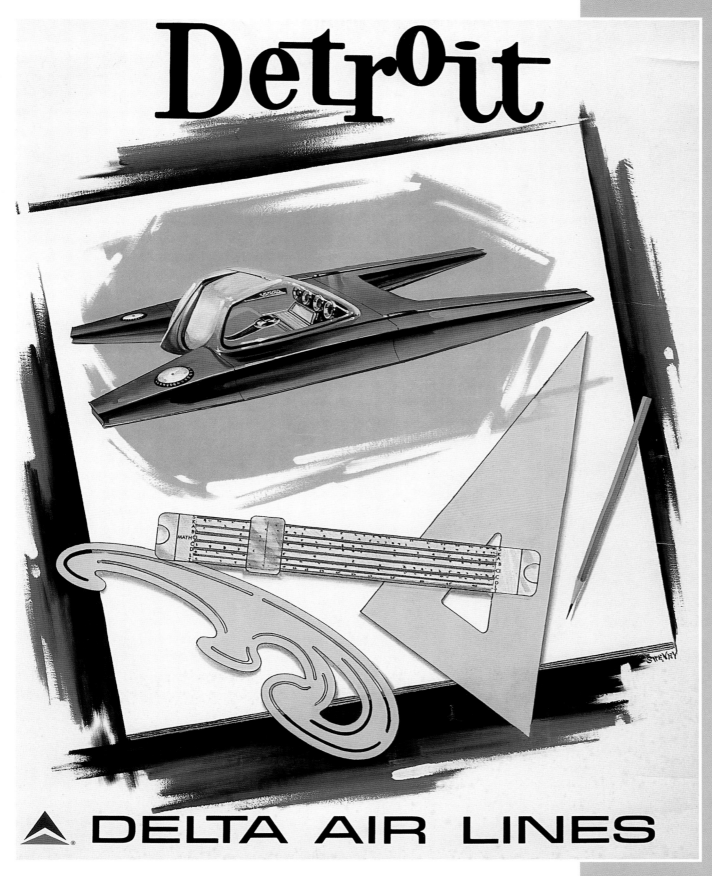

Detroit

Detroit is not often thought of as a poster town, but its industrial base, particularly the auto industry's scope and importance, made it a prime airline destination from the earliest days. Delta's early jet age poster using the slide rule and drafting tools to advocate Detroit's futuristic car designers seems quaint in the computer age.

△ DELTA AIR LINES

This was one of TWA's last posters, an unwitting memorial now to a fine American airline and a tragedy that reaches far beyond America. But memory of rich achievements is ultimately inspiring, a solid foundation for recovery and adventures to come if sought with the visionary commitment and determination of those who created the world's airlines.

At the close of the last millennium the airlines could look back on over eight decades of history, and could rightly say that the modern airliner was one of the most stunning achievements of the twentieth century. Airline flying has matured into just another safe, swift, reliable, affordable, and all too often gridlocked form of mass transportation. A flight spanning continents is about as exciting as a long ride on a bus. Today we have to look back to sense the thrill of air travel in exotic machines, the delicious tinge of danger aloft, and the rewards of alighting in strange new worlds barely touched by outside influence. Few mementos do it as well as this commemorative retro poster of Hawaiian Airlines.

Aeroflot Li-2, 48, 104

Aeropostale, 11, 24, 36, 39, 44, 74

Air Afrique, 48, 52, 74

Air Algerie, 120

Air Canada, 135

Air France, 11, 14, 16, 20, 21, 47, 52, 67, 70, 72, 91, 102, 126, 138, 147

Air Jamaica, 171

Air Orient, 11, 37, 70

Air Transport Command, 86, 112

Air Union, 11, 14, 28, 29, 32, 34

Airbus Industrie, 86

Ala Littoria, 65

American Airways, 12, 111, 125, 132

Arpke, Otto, 42

Balbo, Gen. Italo, 40

Baudouin, 149

Beirut, 118

Blitz, Charles, 20

Boeing 307, 58

Boeing 314, 80, 83

Boeing 707, 123, 142

Boeing 727, 155

Boeing 747, 15, 123

Boeing Air Transport, 12

Boeing B-29 Superfortress bomber, 87

Boeing B-377 Stratocruiser, 87, 106, 107, 118

Boeing B-80, 12

Bonacini, 65

Boucher, Lucien, 74

Braniff International Airways, 87, 100, 109, 136, 143

Breguet 280, 29, 34

Breguet XIV, 16, 21

Brenet, S., 82

British Caledonian, 129

British European Airway (BEA), 89

British Overseas Airways Corporation (BOAC), 73, 89, 98, 101, 134

British South American Airways, 87

C-54, 86

Caledonian, 129

Carlin, Jean, 97

Cassandre, 59 See also Mouron, Adolphe

Chanove, P., 67

Chicago World Fair, 40

Chicago, 151

Clipper America, 134, 135

Colin, Paul, 70

Colonial Air Transport, 12, 26

Comet IV, 139

Compagnie des Messageries Aeriennes, 16, 74

Concorde, 86

Continental, 173

Corvair Coronado, 135

Croydon Airport, 10

Curtiss Flying Service, 19

DDL, 95

De Havelland Comet, 134

De Havilland DH 86, 81

DELAG German Airship Transport Company, 10, 14

Delta Airlines, 141, 171

Deutsche Luft Reederei, 11, 13, 23

Deutsche Lufthansa, 11, 23, 25, 60, 69

Dewoitine D338, 72

Dickson, Charles, 71

Dimitri, Ivan, 92

Disney, Walt, 111

Dornier Wal flying boats, 38, 48

Douglas DC-2, 54, 64

Douglas DC-3, 12, 22, 35, 44–46, 58, 64, 72, 78, 86

Douglas DC-4, 49, 86, 90

Douglas DC-6, 87

Douglas DC-6B, 89

Douglas DC-7C, 87, 89

Eastern Air Transport, 12

Ekins, H. R., 46

El Al, 161

Farman F-170 Jabiru airliner, 18

Farman Goliath, 11, 14, 18, 32

Fine, Aaron, 144

Finnair, 170

Flagship New England, 86

Fokker F-13, 27, 35

Fokker Friendship, 140

Fokker F-VIII, 51, 76

Fokker Trimotor, 46

Fokker, Anthony, 12, 22, 64

Ford Trimotor, 12, 26, 35

French Sud Avion Caravelle, 136

Georger, Guy, 162

Golden Gate Bridge, 165

Grace, W. R., 68

Graf Zepplin, 48, 56

Handley Page 0/400, 10, 11, 30

Handley Page Hermes, 101

Handley Page HP-42, 55, 73

Handley Page Transport, 11

Handley Page W-10, 30

Hanscom Field, 86

Hapag Lloyd shipping line, 11

Hawaii, 114

Hawaiian Airlines, 177

Hawaiian Clipper, 46

Heinkel 111, 77

Hindenburg, 46, 48, 56

Hughes, Howard, 142

Iberia, 135

Icelandic Air, 166

Imperial Airways, 11, 30, 48, 49, 53, 62, 71, 73, 75, 79, 89, 101

Japan Air Transport Company, 22
Junker JU-31, 41
Junkers F-13, 11, 25, 33
Junkers G-38, 60
Junkers JU-52, 69
Junkers Luftverkehr, 11
Kauffer, E. McKnight, 113, 128
Klein, David, 135, 142, 145, 148, 154, 155, 160
KLM Royal Dutch Airlines, 11, 46, 47, 51, 62, 108, 132, 135
KNILM, 46
Kuwait Airway, 168
Lawler, P. G., 47, 50, 68, 83
Le Bourget Airport, 10
Lee-Elliot, T., 73
Lignes Aériennes G. Latécoère, 11, 21, 24
Lindbergh, Charles, 12
Lockheed Constellation, 94, 149
Lockheed Electra, 43, 140
Ludenken, Fred, 96
Lufthansa, 11, 41, 48, 69, 77
MAEFORT, 17
Manset, Regis, 102
Martin M-130, 46
MASZOVLET, 104
Maurus, 34
McCarran Airport, 169
Mermoz, Jean, 36, 39
Mexicana, 155
Mouron, Adolphe, 59 See also Cassandre
Nathan, 138
National Air Transport, 12
New Orleans, 141
New Zealand National Airways Corporation, 159
Nielsen, Otto, 116
Northwest Airlines, 43, 106
Northwest Orient, 106, 121
Pago Pago, 83
Paine, Charles, 28
Pan American Airways, 12, 46–50, 54, 57, 58, 63, 66, 68, 80, 85, 87, 88, 90, 97, 112, 114, 127, 137, 146, 174
Pan American Grace Airways (PANAGRA), 54, 68, 143
Pitcairn Aviation, 12
Portez VII, 20
Pursell, Weimer, 119, 125
Quantas Empire Airways, 47, 81, 103, 132, 134
Robertson Airlines, 12
Roquin, 52
Runnells, Clive, 134
Rupp, Gorge, 43
S-40 flying boat, 57
Sabena, 11, 76, 153
Savoia Marchetti, 40, 65, 76

Scandinavian Airlines System, (SAS), 95, 135
Scripps Howard Journal, 46
SIDNA, 11
Sikorsky S-42, 63
Silver City car ferry, 129
Societe Farman, 18
Solon, Albert, 18
South African Airways, 98
Spain, 154
St. Exupery, Antoine, 36
St. Petersburg-Tampa Airboat Line, 10, 11
Staaken bombers, 13
Stark, Freya, 10, 30
Stout, William, 35
Sud Avion Caravelle jet, 86, 147
Suddeutsche Lufthansa, 31
Swiss Air Lines, 11, 78, 135
Swissair, 11, 78, 130
TAP, 163
Tata Airlines, 123
Times Square, 148
"Tin Goose", 12
Trans Australian Airways, 140
Trans World Airlines (TWA), 87, 88, 121, 122, 142, 154, 164, 169, 176
Transcontinental Air Transport, 12, 26
Transcontinental and Western Air (TWA), 12, 58, 94
Trippe, Juan, 134
Tupolev TU-104, 104
UAT, 52
United Airlines, 12, 105, 136, 151
Varig Airlines, 152
Verney Airlines, 12
Vickers Viscount turboprop, 86, 133, 136, 140
Villemot, 99, 110
Von Arenburg, 115
W. R. Grace Company, 54, 143
Western Air Express, 12
Western Airlines, 167
Wibault, Penhoet 28, 61
Wija, Jan, 51, 64
Wootton, Frank, 101
Zepplin airship, 15, 48, 56
Zepplin-Staaken monoplane, 31